# The
# Nanny Factor

## *A Parent's Guide to Finding the Right Nanny for Your Family*

by

D1124284

## Candi Wingate, Founder,
## Nannies4hire.com
## Care4hire.com
## Babysitters4hire.com

Nannies International Press

Published by:  Nannies International Press
                PO Box 2202
                Norfolk, NE 68702
                (402) 379-4121


ISBN-13: 978-0-9826989-0-7

*For my 3 T'S, the lights in my life—*
*my husband Tyler,*
*and our precious sons,*
*Trent and Tyson.*

*Thank you for keeping my life full and my days lively.*

# Acknowledgements

Whether you are running a household or a business, it takes a team to raise a family. My team starts with my parents, Doug and Becky Stevens who really inspire me to be all that I can be. They were self-employed and I grew up watching their hard work, dedication, creativity and tenacity. They were there for me, supporting me when I started my business and encouraging me to pursue my dream.

To my family, my husband Tyler, my sons, Trent and Tyson, and my in-laws Skip and Marilyn Wingate, thank you for your love and support. To the staff at Nannies International, Inc., Anne Rader and Lisa Sterns, thank you for your help each and every day to keep our client families and our nanny candidates happy. Thanks go to our researcher, Maureen O'Crean for finding the facts and figures that tell the story of what it takes to run a family. A special thanks to Sherri Funk from whom I purchased Nannies of Nebraska, which I grew into Nannies4hire.com, Babysitters4hire.com and Care4hire.com.

To all the companies who supported me during the writing of the book, for lending your advice and giving me permission to share your gifts. Thanks to Cheryl Tallman and Joan Ahlers of Fresh Baby for the *All About Me Diary*; to Karmel Publishing, Karen Berg and Melissa Bishop for their book, *The Caregiver's Organizer for My Child*. Thanks to Sarah Ban Breathnach and Simple Abundance for the use of the excerpt from her book, *The Victorian Nursery Companion*. Thanks to Sherri Services, the International Nannies Association and Michelle LaRowe for their advice. Thanks to Guy Maddalone and Lara Spendiff at GTM Household Employment Experts for their advice on the regulations and laws on hiring a nanny and nanny payroll. Thanks to

Sue Balcer at JustYourType.biz for taking my words and making them look wonderful on the page.

And last, but certainly not least, a deep-felt thank you to my personal nannies, today and over the years, who have been such a support in keeping our sons happy and healthy and to all our computer programmers, for keeping our business running smoothly. I couldn't have done this without all of your help and support.

# Table of Contents

# INTRODUCTION: The Origin of the Nanny

While it may seem like the rise in the employment of nannies is an occurrence of the late 20<sup>th</sup> and early 21<sup>st</sup> Century, nothing can be farther from the truth. The use of nannies in the home began well over 100 years ago. In her book, **The Victorian Nursery Companion,** author Sarah Ban Breathnach shares with us the beginnings of childcare in the home:

*The concept of the nursery—a separate part of the house reserved for the children and presided over by a nurse or "nanny"—was the creation of Victorian Britain. The Industrial Revolution brought about many social and economic changes and one of them was the new wealth of the burgeoning middle classes between 1870 and 1890 who sought to emulate the lifestyle of the upper classes.*

*By 1890 the presence of Nanny in the home had become an institution in British society. So entrenched was Nanny's role in the physical and emotional rearing of a generation of children that the respected English household authority Cassell's felt compelled to comment that, 'Under ordinary circumstances the mother is the rightful guardian of the nursery and no one can properly fill her place. ... For no matter how clever a nurse may be, a mother has no right to put the entire control of the children into her hands.'*

*Nevertheless, middleclass and wealthy Victorian English parents did for the most part surrender complete control of their children to Nanny. The children's nurse was expected to feed, bathe, dress and toilet train her young charges, teach them manners and morals, entertain and discipline them and stand in as a surrogate parent for babies and young children until they grew old enough to be sent away to boarding school at age seven for boys, or if they were girls, to be instructed at home by a governess. Even then, Nanny remained as the dominant presence in their lives until the children officially graduated from the nursery at the onset of adolescence. It was Nanny who got up with the children at night if they were sick or frightened, saw baby's first steps, wrote them encouraging letters to assuage their home sickness, and it was Nanny to whom countless Victorian children came to depend upon, trust and love.*

*Middleclass Victorian American families, on the other hand, tended to have mother raise the children with the occasional help of a mother's assistant who did not live in the house but came daily.*

With the changes in our families and the rise of two working parents, it seems today that a nanny is an indispensible aide to raising happy and healthy children. Within the pages of this book, I hope to share my knowledge and experience with you on how a nanny can be an asset to your family today.

Candi Wingate

*Section One*

# What Is a Nanny?

one

# De-Bunking the Nanny Myths

If you just read the headlines in American pop culture, you would get the wrong idea about nannies. With books and movies like *The Nanny Diaries*, lawsuits between celebrity couples and their nanny, or an affair between the nanny and the husband, you might want to run away from the idea of a nanny. The truth is that just like a reality show, what you see is not really what is going on. Millions of families are enjoying the privilege and responsibility of working with a nanny without a scandal. You can too.

In today's society there are many benefits of hiring a nanny:

1. If you have two or more children, it may be cost effective for you to hire a nanny, as many daycares could cost you more.

2. If your child is sick, you can still go to work as the nanny can stay home with the child.

3. A nanny can simplify your life. For example, a nanny can be an extra pair of hands helping with household duties, laundry, errands, transporting children and starting the evening meal. This allows for more quality family time when the parents arrive home.

4. Many families are using "nanny share". This is when two families share one nanny. This cuts down on cost but you still experience the benefit of having a nanny.

5. No need to rush in the morning to get the children out the door for daycare or school. A nanny is an extra pair of hands in the morning.

We're going to take some time to breakdown some popular myths about nannies. In January of 2010, we asked the families who use nannies through Nannies4hire.com to complete a survey about how the economic downturn was affecting their families. We are using the data gathered to answer some of the myths about nannies.

## Myth #1. Nannies are for the wealthy — FALSE

The federal government has identified income of $250,000 a year as the threshold for the wealthy. When families with nannies were asked how much their family income was, 34% earned less than $100,000 per year, 22% earned between $100,000 and $150,000, 17.5% earned between $150,000 and $200,000, and 31% earned over $200,000. Working families are the ones most using nannies. (N=796[1], 33% did not answer the question).

## Myth #2. A nanny must work full-time — FALSE

The nanny's schedule works around the schedule of the family. Of the families who responded to our surveys,

---

1 N refers to the number of people who answered a particular question. It changes from question to question.

46.9% of the nannies worked part-time, with a range of hours per week varying from under 10 to 30. You will be able to find a high quality nanny who can work with your schedule.

## Myth #3.  A nanny must make a year commitment — FALSE

The only legally binding agreement between a nanny and a family is a written contract that outlines all the terms of their agreement. When we asked the nannies (January, 2010 N=761) registered with Nannies4hire.com if they had a written contract, only 26% have a contract with their employer. This is not the case with an AU PAIR, however, which does require a 12 month commitment for a J-1 visa.

## Myth #4.  A nanny is not safe — FALSE

In a study of Healthy Steps for Young Children[2], the leading cause of injury to children was related to the family, not the nanny. Children of unmarried parents were the most likely to be injured. The conclusion of the study was, "Household composition seems to play a key role in placing children at risk for medically attended injuries." In a study that compared children who received home care, center-based care, and other forms of out-of-home child care, the rate of minor injuries was highest in center-based care, but there was not a significant difference among the

---

2 A program of The Commonwealth Fund in conjunction with Boston University School of Medicine: National Evaluation. Co-sponsored by the American Academy of Pediatrics

three types of care for severe injuries." *(PEDIATRICS Vol. 122 No. 5 November 2008, pp. e980-e987)*

## Myth #5.  A nanny will invade your privacy — FALSE

In today's society, most nannies live outside of their employers' homes. When we asked our nannies, only 18% lived in the home, and 81% lived in their own home (N=761). Even though 57% of the nannies reported they feel as if they are appreciated by the family, it is the parents' responsibility to set and keep the privacy boundaries intact.

## Myth #6.  A nanny will only take care of the children (no housework, cooking, etc.) — FALSE

A nanny is an asset to a family and, in most cases, will help your house run smoothly. The most important criterion is not to burden a nanny with non-child related activities and detract from their primary responsibility: the care of your child. Seventy-seven percent of the nannies who responded to our first survey in 2009 are doing child-related activities (homework, errands, birthday parties, housework, laundry, and meal preparation), while 19% are involved in family duties. To break it down even further, 34% do housekeeping for the family, and 59% do housekeeping for the children, 77% prepare meals for the children only, and 20% prepare the meals for the whole family. In 2010, 79% are doing more than just watching children. When you get ready to hire your nanny, see how your nanny can help your family as a whole.

## Myth #7. I will not know what is going on in my home with a nanny — FALSE

Working with a nanny is not a mystery. By setting up your communication systems at the start of your relationship, you will know everything that your child did that day. We recommend keeping a nanny journal, a daily reporting book where your nanny records important milestones, successes and challenges of the day. Seeing that your house is neat and clean, and that your child is happy, those are the best measures of your nanny's progress. (More on nanny cams later in the book.)

## Myth #8. With a nanny, your child will not socialize with other children — FALSE

A major portion of a nanny's duty is to supervise your child's social interactions with other children. Whether it is a play date with friends, birthday parties, organized sports activities, or fun at the park, your nanny is your representative with your child. Whatever is important to you is important to your nanny.

## Myth #9. Hiring a nanny is too complicated — FALSE

Hiring a qualified nanny is easier than you think. With an online database service like Nannies4hire.com, you can preview available nannies in your zip code in the comfort of your own home. You will see their picture, experience, health status, education, and more. After you have narrowed your selection to two or three prospects, take advantage of the tools (for example, sample texts such as the nanny contract that can be found in the Appendix) that will give you peace of mind when hiring a nanny to care for your child.

## Myth #10. If I hire a nanny and am not happy with the relationship, I am stuck — FALSE

Working with a nanny is no different than your own relationship at work. As the employer, you have goals and expectations you have shared with your nanny. One way to be clear on this is to develop a written job description, or adapt one from the sample contract in the Appendix so you and your nanny are on the same page. We recommend at least a three month introductory period so that you and your nanny can see if it is a good fit. In any event, if you are not happy with your nanny's performance, it is not an emotional issue. You deserve the best nanny for your child . . . with no reservations.

## Candi's Take on Stay-At-Home Moms Versus Working Moms

The debate over whether mothers should work is an emotionally-charged debate that has left mothers on both sides of the aisle feeling judged and undervalued. As more and more women become working mothers, the debate intensifies. In 1965, 33% of moms worked outside the home. Today, 71% of moms work outside the home. Now, more than ever, we, as women, need to come together, to reinforce our right to make the choice that's right for our families, and to reinforce the rights of others to do likewise even if that choice differs from our own. Let us acknowledge that there is no "right" or "wrong" answer here, and that difficult decisions are made more difficult when criticized by others.

Some moms prefer to stay at home. Some moms prefer to work outside the home. Children tend to thrive in happy environments. Thus, there is a potential advantage to the children if mom works outside the home . . . if that makes the mom a happier mom.

Some moms who prefer to stay at home simply do not have that option. Women who work outside the home are not doing it to buy that next Lexus or keep up with the Joneses. More than likely, she is working to put the next meal on the table or to keep a roof over the family's heads. Children tend to thrive in environments in which their basic needs are met.

A working mom is not necessarily putting work ahead of her children: she may be working to help support and care for her children. Thus, working is not inconsistent with putting her children first in her life. Studies have shown that children of working moms will do better on social and cognitive tests than will their counterparts raised by stay-at-home moms if the children of working mom have been placed in high quality childcare.

The guilt associated with perceived child abandonment or neglect must be wrestled with by ferreting out the logic in the emotion. The maternal instinct to nurture children is powerful, but nurturing must be construed to include providing those children with shelter, food, and the material things the children need to attend to their daily lives. These objects are achieved, many times, by moms working outside the home. In all aspects of life, there are trade-offs. Moms experience a number of trade-offs when choosing to stay at home or work outside the home. One of the primary trade-offs in that choice is income to fund the family or time with the family. It is a difficult decision that each mom must make based on her own unique circumstances. Let us each make the decision that we feel is best for our families, and let us each validate the choices of other. By doing so, everyone wins: moms, children, and society.

# What a Nanny Is and What She Is Not

Wouldn't it be wonderful for a singing, flying and magical being like Mary Poppins to drop into your home? What about a tough, no-nonsense approach like Supernanny Jo Frost when it comes to raising children? Fantasy aside, real families need someone who cares about the well-being of children. What every parent wants is the best of all worlds for their children. Here are some definitions to help you navigate the childcare world:

NANNY: a committed childcare provider, employed by a family to provide supervision and a nurturing environment for the family's children, without direct parental supervision. A nanny may live in or out of a family's primary residence and is focused on the needs of the child. The well-being, education and development of the child on a day-to-day basis is the primary responsibility of the nanny. Duties that are required for the care of a child such as bathing, meal preparation, laundry, housekeeping, homework supervision, errands, exercise, and transportation are part of a nanny's responsibility. Formal education is not required if the nanny has suitable experience with children. It is recommended that all nannies and childcare providers be certified in infant and child CPR.

**MOTHER'S HELPER:** The biggest difference between a mother's helper and nanny or au pair is one of supervision. A mother's helper works under the direct supervision of the parent and is not responsible for the children on her own. Her decision-making authority is limited. A mother's helper is often a younger woman, in her teens, who may want to be a caregiver in the future. She is not expected to have the knowledge or experience of a caregiver who calls herself a nanny or a babysitter.

**BABY NURSE:** Contrary to the title, a baby nurse is not a medical professional, but an expert in the needs of healthy newborns. One of the functions of a baby nurse is to educate new parents in the care of the infant. A baby nurse will work as a day nurse or a night nurse, but not both. If you want 24 hours of support, you will want two baby nurses, each working a 12 hour shift. In the first few weeks of the child's life, the baby nurse will take over the tasks of feeding, bathing, and diaper changes so the new mother can get her rest. If a mother is breastfeeding, a baby nurse supports the process and allows the mother to get rest between feedings. Newborns will need care for their healing umbilical cords and circumcision sites. The baby nurse will teach the new parents to understand the needs of the infant, including burping, swaddling, and creating a feeding and sleeping schedule for newborns.

**BABYSITTER:** A temporary childcare provider who provides care of children, without direct parental supervision, in the family home. A babysitter works for short periods of time, and the primary responsibility is the care and entertainment of children when the parents are not at home. A babysitter's responsibility will change from situation to situation depending on the need of the child during the span of time that the babysitter is to provide care.

**AU PAIR:** A foreign young person, between the ages of 18-26, who comes to the United States to live with a family. Unlike a nanny, an au pair does require a commitment of 12 months. There are many requirements for the au pair visa, which is required for an au pair coming into the US. There are also fees that run between $5,000-$7,000 that must be paid in addition to a $500 educational stipend and weekly 'pocket money' expense of approximately $175.00. Au pairs are limited to attending to no more than four children from the ages of three months to 12 years. Families must go through one of 11 designated au pair agencies to obtain a J-1 au pair visa. Please check with the US Department of State for details.

**MANNY:** The term indicates a male who is performing traditional nanny duties. As roles of men and women change in society, the recognition of the benefits of a strong male role model in a child's life has given way to more respect for males in traditional 'female' work. A manny may be especially helpful with boys and girls who do not have a father in their lives.

**GOVERNESS:** A committed childcare provider, employed by a family to provide supervision and education for the family's school-aged children, without direct parental supervision. A governess may live in or out of a family's primary residence. The education and development of the child on a day-to-day basis is the primary responsibility of the governess.

## Candi's Take on Hiring a Manny
## or Male Nanny

Remember that episode of *Friends* when Rachel hires a male babysitter for baby Emma, and Ross is stunned by her decision? When most people think of nannies, they usually think of females, who are considered to be caring, nurturing and, well, maternal. But many males thrive in caretaking roles - as teachers, coaches, mentors and nannies. If you're looking to hire a nanny, consider what qualities are most important to you. For instance:

- If you're a single mother, you might want to hire a male nanny to serve as a consistent and positive male role model.
- If your child is athletic and interested in sports, consider a nanny who shares those same interests. Your football-obsessed young son might enjoy having a male nanny who was a football player or a young woman who loves the game.
- If you have daughters who are into princesses and fairy tales, a male nanny might not be the best choice for them, or they might enjoy having a "prince" to join their princess games. (I know plenty of dads, uncles, and other men who patiently have tea parties or get their hair styled by the little ladies in their lives.)

There are many things to consider that are clearly more important than your nanny's gender. Is the nanny candidate kind to your child? Do you trust them? Do they have excellent experience and references? Is the candidate smart and responsible? Does your child like them? Will they do the things your child enjoys, whether that's building forts, playing tag, or doing craft projects? If so, hire the person, regardless of gender.

# The Role of a Nanny:
# Family Member or Employee?

Trying to decide if your nanny is an employee or family member is a no-win game. For a truly rich and rewarding experience with your nanny, she must be both. It is much like the introduction of a young woman's suitor to the family. At first, the young man is held at arm's length until he demonstrates his worthiness to be a member of the family. Once he proves his worth, and the wedding takes place, he becomes a member of the family.

When you are hiring a nanny, it is important to keep it a business transaction. You are, after all, inviting a stranger into your home to have access to your most precious of all gifts, your child. She may seem nice, but like a true suitor, she must earn your respect. Hiring your nanny is an intellectual process: setting up the job description; agreeing to the job description; checking references; performing a background check on their driving record, criminal history, and verifying any educational qualifications; negotiating salary; and a performance test. You handle all of these tasks with the business-oriented, logical, left side of your brain. Once your nanny candidates pass this rigorous test, the really hard part begins: the emotional test.

When a nanny starts to interact with your child, both your heart and your mind become involved. You want your child to enjoy being with their nanny. You want them to feel respect, admiration and be treated with love each and every day. You want them to know and understand boundaries, to have successes, and to build self-respect. A child knows when he or she is not loved, so the interaction of your child and nanny must be loving. Over time, you and your child will build attachments to your nanny. It is a natural process and one that is important, with one caveat. Your nanny is not actually a member of your family.

How your nanny sees her role in the family comes entirely from you. If you set good boundaries and keep to them, you can keep the correct balance in your relationship. If you cross those boundaries, gossip with your nanny, do 'favors', lend money, or socialize without the children, you are asking for trouble. How you conduct yourself in your relationship with your nanny determines the separation between your personal business and the business of the care of your child.

## The Nanny Relationships in Your Family

The relationship with a nanny is dependent upon the person with whom she is interacting. With the wife and mother, a nanny will usually have a closer and warmer relationship than with a husband and father. Gender roles and energy are usually what defines the relationship you will have with your nanny. Women, feminine energy, tend to care for and nurture their families, while men, masculine energy, provide for and protect their families. Now don't get mad at me yet; I'm just sharing my 25 years of experience with you. As you look at your family, assign the male and female roles in your household without judgment. This will help you understand the differences between you and your spouse, no matter which one of you is reading this book. One of you will see the nanny as a family member and one of you will see the nanny as an employee. Understanding this type of role assignment now will keep you from having many arguments in the future. It is just the nature of the intimate relationship you have with this person who cares for your child.

Whichever parent is the primary caregiver will have a closer, more personal relationship with the nanny. That parent will see and interact with the nanny every day and will tend, over time, to see the nanny as a member of the family. The parent who works long hours outside of the home and is not hands-on in the care of the children is usually the masculine energy. This parent will tend to see the nanny relationship from a business point of view. To this parent, the nanny will be an employee.

Remembering that your nanny is not your friend or family member, even if you get along well, is important to the integrity of your child's experience with your nanny. If you run into any issues, separating the employment relationship from the family-like relationship will help you clear up any confusion. The following activity will help you keep your two worlds operating smoothly.

**Activity #1: Is your nanny a friend or employee:**

**Here are a few of the behaviors of a friend: Add some of your own.**

1. Shares personal information with each other.

2. Does favors for each other equally.

3. Can call on in a time of need.

4.  Socializes outside of work and the home together.

5.  Builds a relationship of trust by mutual experiences.

6.  _____

7.  _____

8.  _____

9.  _____

10._____

## Here are some behaviors of an employee: Add your own.

1.  Arrives at work at the designated time.

2.  Completes specific tasks as directed.

3.  Reports any problems or issues that arise when trying to complete tasks.

4.  All work is subject to evaluation by the employer.

5.  Does not make independent decisions regarding the well-being of the children.

6.  _____

7.  _____

8.  _____

9.  _____

10._____

## Who is your nanny to your child?

Outside of the child's parents, the nanny becomes the most important person in the child's life. As a child begins to trust and rely on the nanny, it is natural for them to fall in love with the nanny. It is part of a child's loving and inclusive nature. Remember that your nanny is your partner in raising a happy and healthy child and is not taking anything away from you and your relationship. A child sees their parents in a special light, and nothing can replace this primary relationship in their heart. It is important for your child to be vulnerable to the nanny. That is the only way that your child will learn to have healthy relationships. So, remember that your nanny is your stand-in. Thus, your nanny should reflect your values, morals, and beliefs, because all your nanny can pass on to your child is what your nanny believes.

four

# Where Does Your Nanny Live?

One of the important issues in hiring your nanny is where she will live. Even though the thought of a 24-hour back-up plan may intrigue you, a live-in nanny is still entitled to overtime pay for working over 40 hours in a week. However, the most important cost to your family is not money. It is the potential loss of intimacy and privacy with your family. When a nanny lives in, the boundaries between family member and employee can get blurred.

## Live-in Nanny – Things to Consider

A live-in nanny is not as popular as it once was. When Nannies4hire. com surveyed our nanny database in January, 2010, over 3,387 nannies gave us the inside scoop on what's going on in the nanny industry. Here are some of the facts as a point of reference for you:

| | |
|---|---|
| Live In Nanny | 19.4% |
| Live Out Nanny | 80.6%  (N=3,037) |

If you do decide to have a live-in nanny, here are some of the important matters to consider.

- **Housing:** A live-in nanny needs her own room and access to a bathroom.

- **Work schedule:** Make sure you have your nanny's work schedule outlined in the employment contract. If you have a flexible work schedule, a weekly schedule or preferably a two week schedule should be agreed upon with your nanny.

- **Labor hours:** Check with your state to see how many hours constitute a full-time work week. As a general rule 35-40 hours is considered full-time, but this is governed state-by-state.

- **Days off:** Your nanny should receive two consecutive days off each week, even if you need her to work weekends, unless you agree to a different schedule.

- **Nanny's privacy:** With live-in help, it is important to provide your nanny with privacy and downtime when she is off-duty. This is an important consideration, and you should ensure that your child understands that even though the nanny is in the house, she is off limits.

- **Transportation:** Some families may provide a car for the nanny's use if she does not have a car and insurance of her own. If you expect your nanny to provide transportation for your child, gas, mileage, and wear and tear on her car should be in your contract. Also, if your child needs a car seat, an additional car seat may be provided for the nanny's car.

## Live-out Nanny – Things to Consider

With a nanny that lives outside your home, reliability becomes your number one consideration. If you have to be at your office by a designated time, you want to make sure that the nanny you hire is dependable, both in her personal characteristics, as well as her transportation. Here are some important considerations:

- **Work schedule:** Make sure that you add in extra time in the morning shift so you will have ample time to get to work.

- **Readiness:** Your nanny should arrive at your home, showered, dressed and ready to work from the time she arrives.

- **Hours:** Remember full-time is 8 hours a day and 30 hours a week in some states, while it is 40 hours a week in others. Make sure you check with your state's labor department for the correct information in your state. If you work a 9 to 5 job plus transportation time, you already have a 10-12 hour shift depending on your commute.

- **Salary vs. Hourly:** You may have an option to pay a salary if you have a live-in nanny, but employment issues such as hourly wages, minimum wages, and overtime pay must comply with both state and federal minimum wage. Overtime does apply to any employee who works over 40 hours in a week. The overtime pay is time and one-half of the hourly wages paid. Under the Fair Labor Standards Act (FLSA), the federal minimum wage is $7.25 (as of 1/1/2010). You must also check your state/local government in the event that they require greater wages than the federal rate. Please consult http://www.dol.gov/esa/minwage/america.htm for information in your state.

- **Employment records:** As the employer, you are required to maintain records of employment. These records include the employee's name, address, age, Social Security number or green card information, wages, hours worked, and days worked each week. Please contact the US Department of Labor at www.dol.gov for more information.
  http://www.dol.gov/whd/regs/compliance/whdfs22.pdf

- **Full-Time vs. Part-Time:** It is important to hire and work with a nanny that can work with your schedule. A full-time nanny generally works 40 hours a week and a part-time nanny generally works from 1 day to 32 hours a week, depending on your state's employment guidelines. If your child is in school but you want your nanny to be on-call, you may want to hire a nanny-housekeeper. This joint job title would provide benefits to your household while providing paid work time to your nanny.

- **Nanny share:** Sometimes families in close proximity to each other may try to share one nanny. Both families would be hiring one person to share two jobs. In this case, it is really important for the buyer to beware—a nanny can only go to one place at a time if there is a breakdown in schedules or an emergency. Another alternative is to have a nanny go to one house and care for all the children together.

# The Gift of a Nanny

There are very few occupations in life that require the gift of love as a job requirement. Nannies must love children first and foremost, and love your child in particular. A child knows if they are accepted for who they are, and there is no more important person in your child's life (after you and your spouse) than your nanny.

Once you have decided on the hours, wages, and the details that define a job, the real work begins. Having a nanny is a gift of security and peace of mind, knowing that your child is safe, healthy and happy. For your child, a nanny is a companion, playmate, disciplinarian, tutor, coach and friend. You will probably never experience a closer, more intimate relationship with an employee than you will with your nanny.

The role of a nanny is to bond with your child. It is a natural process: your child will normally become attached to your nanny. It is important for you not to be threatened by this relationship. You will always be the parent, and your child's strongest bond is with you.

Since a child is dependent on his or her nanny for survival, the elements of trust, reliability, stability and love should be present in daily interactions. So, the selection process of the nanny is your number one priority. It is important that you and your nanny share the same values and ideals on the issues most important to you. We asked our nannies (N=1,913) what they thought were good parenting traits in the families that they worked for. Here are some of the more frequent responses:

- Being involved with the child even though the parents work a lot.

- Being concerned about who is caring for their child.

- Putting the child's needs first.

- Showing consistent, loving discipline.

- Making time to eat dinner with their child.

- Knowing their child's likes, dislikes, fears, concerns.

- Using creative ways of learning, being involved, and active parenting.

- Giving guidance that is consistent with both love, affection, and discipline.

- Listening to their child and being encouraging, patient, and understanding.

- Saying how proud they are of their child when they do something good.

- Always saying that they love the child.

- Always caring about their child's manners.

By working as a team with your nanny, you will share in the joys of a happy, healthy and enthusiastic child, ready to embrace a full life.

## Candi's Take on Nanny Envy – What If They Love Her Too Much?

When you hire a nanny, you check her background, references, and experience. You want the perfect person to care for your child: someone that your child will love and want to spend time with. But what if they love her too much?

It's not unusual for mothers to feel threatened by, and envious of, their nannies. It's often difficult to leave your child to go to work, and here's this "other woman" who gets to do all of the fun stuff that you're missing, like playing with your child, teaching them new things, even being there for their milestones. Talk about major mommy guilt! It's natural to feel possessive and protective of your child: that's the maternal instinct. It's also OK to need help with childcare, it takes a village to raise a child, right?

But hiring a nanny, which is supposed to make your life easier, can be complicated, as you may struggle with the unique dynamic of this relationship. You're having an intensely intimate relationship with your employee: she has become an instant part of your family. She sees you at your most vulnerable i.e., in your bathrobe after a sleepless night with a sick baby, she gets a glimpse into your personal life, such as seeing that your house is always messy, and she's sharing the most personal and familiar routines with your child. She's comforting your child when they are hurt or scared, cheering for successes, and doing all of the other things that you would do if you were there.

While you may feel conflicted or upset that your child loves your nanny so much, it's actually a *good* thing. Don't you want your child to feel comfortable with their childcare provider?

You aren't the only mom to feel *nanny envy*. You're also not the only mom to feel guilty about working, not keeping a spotless house, not baking bread from scratch, and the list goes on. Give yourself a break, do the best you can, and count on help from others including your nanny, who really does have your family's best interests at heart.

*Section Two*

# Discovering the Nanny That's Right for You

# The Nanny Match Game

Bringing a person into your home, especially to care for your child, is a big responsibility, to yourself and your child. Can you picture that another adult will be guiding your child in those moment-by-moment decisions for eight to ten hours a day? Of course, there are many things for you to consider as you look to hire your nanny. The most important of these considerations is to find a nanny who shares your values. When you and your nanny share the same values, you will have peace of mind that your child will be raised by your guidelines.

We all like to strive to be open and accepting of cultures and beliefs that are different from our own. When it comes to a primary influence in the upbringing of our children, we need to go a little deeper.

One way to determine the values that are important to you is to make a list of your top ten values, and then identify your deal breakers. We suggest that you have your nanny applicants also complete the values identification process. It will be easy for you to spot those candidates that are right for your family and those who are not a good match because of basic differences. It is also important to note that you cannot discriminate against any potential employees according to the federal equal employment opportunity laws:

## *Federal Equal Employment Opportunity (EEO) Laws*

### What Are the Federal Laws Prohibiting Employment Discrimination?

- Title VII of the Civil Rights Act of 1964 (Title VII), which prohibits employment discrimination based on race, color, religion, sex, or national origin;

- the Pregnancy Discrimination Act of 1978, which prohibits employment discrimination based on pregnancy, childbirth, or related medical conditions;

- the Equal Pay Act of 1963 (EPA), which protects men and women who perform substantially equal work in the same establishment from sex-based wage discrimination;

- the Immigration Reform and Control Act of 1986, which prohibits employment discrimination based on citizenship or immigration status;

- the Age Discrimination in Employment Act of 1967 (ADEA), which protects individuals who are 40 years of age or older;

- Title I and Title V of the Americans with Disabilities Act of 1990 (ADA), which prohibit employment discrimination against qualified individuals with disabilities;

- Sections 501 and 505 of the Rehabilitation Act of 1973, which prohibit discrimination against qualified individuals with disabilities who work in the federal government; and

- the Genetic Information Non-Discrimination Act of 2008, which prohibits employment discrimination based on genetic information.[3]

Your home state may have laws which also apply. To make the process a little easier for you, we have identified those different areas of life that may make a difference to you and your child. Don't make yourself crazy here; just remember what is important to you. You will narrow the focus in the next exercise.

Step One is to review the list of values below and check off the values most important to you. To make it easier to identify, they are organized by category. You may want to add one of your own. Take a few minutes to review these value groupings: Character, Personal, Social, Political, and Cultural.

Once you know your own values and those of your potential nannies, you can deal with any differences in an open and honest way. By requesting that your nanny follows your value structure in dealing with your child, you will avoid possible problems in the future.

---

3 Source: *The U.S. Equal Employment Opportunity Commission* (Nov, 2009)

| VALUES IDENTIFICATION — CHARACTER | |
|---|---|
| | Not Important |
| | Honest |
| | Dependable |
| | Punctual |
| | Trustworthy |
| | Respectful |
| | Responsible |
| | Caring |
| | Clean |
| | Organized |
| | Patient |
| | Compassionate |
| | Kind |
| | Committed |
| | Positive |
| | Loyal |
| | Generous |
| | Self-Respecting |
| | Self-Disciplined |
| | Integrity |
| | Cooperative |

| VALUES IDENTIFICATION — MONEY | |
|---|---|
| | Not Important |
| | Thrifty |
| | Charitable |
| | Frugal |
| | Generous |
| | Hard-Working |
| | Independent |
| | Resourceful |
| | Responsible |
| | Selfish |
| | Cost-Conscious |
| | Fiscally Extravagant |
| | Budget-Minded |

| VALUES IDENTIFICATION — PERSONAL | |
|---|---|
| | Green Living |
| | Recycling |
| | Diet – Traditional |
| | Diet – Vegetarian |
| | Diet – Organic |
| | Exercise Level |
| | Other |

| VALUES IDENTIFICATION – CULTURAL ISSUES ||
|---|---|
| | Keeping Cultural Traditions |
| | Preparing Cultural Foods |
| | Wearing Cultural Clothing |
| | Studying Cultural Practices |
| | Socializing With Members Of My Culture |

seven

# Understanding the Needs of Your Family

One of the joys of being a parent is watching your child grow and change. As your child changes, so does the skill set you need from your nanny. Of course, there are some timeless qualities that you hope all of your nannies may possess: a compassionate and loving nature, patience, and creativity, to name a few. Let's take a quick look at your child's developmental stages to understand what type of nanny you need in the early years.

### Newborns: Birth to Three Months

In the weeks following the birth of your child, you may think that all you do is feed, diaper, and watch your baby sleep. Very quickly, this will end, and you will see some changes. During this period of time, infants develop stronger motor skills, including holding their head up while lying on their stomach, kicking more vigorously, and grasping a toy. *(Mayo Clinic – © 1998-2009 Mayo Foundation for Medical Education and Research (MFMER))*

During this brief period of time, the nanny provides the parents with the time and space to rest and recover from the birth. An attentive and knowledgeable baby nurse will help you easily make the transition from newborn to infant. A baby nurse is usually hired for a specific period of time after a child is born. Make sure you discuss this during your interviews with the baby nurse applicants so you can plan for a transition.

### Infants: Four Months to 12 Months

You are going to be amazed at how quickly your child's world changes as early as four months. Instead of being internally focused, your baby now has a larger world perspective. The senses of hearing and sight become stronger, and your interaction with your baby becomes more personable. The smiles and babbling now have a new meaning: the baby is interacting with you. Increased motor skills show up as rolling over, lifting of the head and even crawling motions may begin to emerge. Of course, every baby develops skills at their own pace, so don't compare your baby's progress to your neighbor's child.

With clearer vision and hearing, it is time to start interacting and stimulating your baby. Talking, music, and reading are great to support your child's development. It is also very important that your baby is touched and cuddled. *(© 1998-2009 Mayo Foundation for Medical Education and Research (MFMER))*

With each monthly milestone, your infant will continue to grow and develop strength and motor skills. You will want to hire a nanny who is experienced with infants for the first year so you will have an additional resource tracking your infant's development.

### Toddler Development

As your infant moves into the toddler stage, usually between one and three years of age, your nanny needs to be equipped with patience and discernment. During this stage of child development, toddlers are developing their motor skills, learning to walk before they talk, and developing their desire for independence. Often labeled the Terrible Two's, these toddlers aren't really terrible; they are active and on-the-go. With their new found mobility in walking and running, they have become the explorers of their new world. Add to this the favorite word of toddlers, "No", and one of the most important issues that will confront your nanny is discipline.

By clearly defining a plan of discipline with your nanny, you remain in control of your toddler's development. Are you a believer in self-expression or do you want your child to closely follow adult direction? During this time of curiosity and exploration, you want to be on the same page with your nanny and trust her judgment when you are not home. Knowing what is important to you is the first step to raising a happy toddler.

## Pre-school and Beyond

During the first five years of life, children need continued supervision during their waking hours. The energy, discipline, encouragement, play, and social interaction your child receives is important to their fundamental development of physical, emotional, and mental skills. Just as a child changes and grows, so may the skills needed by your nanny change. Depending on your family's needs, you will want to think about the pros and cons of hiring a nanny that is experienced with your child's age and developmental needs. By building a length of time into your contracts, you allow yourself the ability to change nannies without guilt as the needs of your family change.

## A Note on Spirited and High Needs Children

If you are the parent of a spirited or high needs child, you already know that your child requires more time, understanding, nurturing, and supervision. Your nanny is your partner in understanding and helping your spirited child grow into a responsible and mature adult. There are some foundational books that have been written that explain the characteristics of the spirited child and how to meet these challenges. These books include: *Raising Your Spirited Child* by Mary Sheedy Kurcinka, *Living with the Alert Active Child* by Linda S. Budd, *The Difficult Child* by Dr. Stanley Turecki, and *Parenting the Fussy Baby and the High Needs Child* by Martha Sears and Dr. William Sears. Each of these books looks at the spirited child at different stages of development.

The characteristics of the spirited child were first identified in a 30 year longitudinal study started in 1956 by Alexander Thomas, Stella Chess and Herbert Birch.

The "Spirited Child" main characteristics are:

**INTENSITY:** the spirited child is loud and prone to drama outside themselves, and quiet and internally observant – with an inward focus on themselves,

**PERSISTENCE:** the spirited child is occasionally quite focused on an idea or goal, such that it is difficult to change their mind,

**SENSITIVITY:** the environment can easily over-stimulate the spirited child, and many have a low sensory threshold to any of the five senses, such as sounds that are too loud,

**PERCEPTIVENESS:** the spirited child may pay attention to everything happening in their environment, become easily distracted, and lose their focus,

**ADAPTIBILITY:** the spirited child has difficulty changing from one activity to another,

**REGULARITY:** the spirited child doesn't have natural schedules for eating or sleeping,

**ENERGY:** the spirited child is high energy, physically active, and very curious in exploring their environment,

**FIRST REACTION:** the spirited child may withdraw when introduced to new things, and

**MOOD:** the spirited child has frequent, unpredictable mood swings.

A child who is identified as spirited exhibits these characteristics frequently in daily life. In reporting their findings in *Principles and Practices of Child Psychiatry* by Stella Chase, M.D. and Mahin Hassibi, M.D., "childcare practices, to be successful, must differ for different children." It is estimated that 20% of children will be identified as spirited or high needs, so this is an important area to discuss prior to hiring a nanny.

In our survey of nannies and babysitters, 27% (N=840) reported that they care for children with behavior problems. Many of the nannies reported the characteristics of spirited children, without identifying that these children needed special consideration. In some instances, the parents did not share with the nanny that the children required more time, nurturing, and understanding. These nannies quit within a few weeks, causing disruption to the child's routine. By sharing with the nanny candidates during the interviews that your child is spirited, you will find the right nanny for your child.

## A Note on Special Needs Children

Nannies4hire.com has extensive experience matching nannies with special needs children. Whether your child has a physical, mental, developmental, or emotional disability, or a combination of these, we're confident that we can find the right nanny to care for your exceptional child.

When considering a nanny, parents of a special needs child need to ask specific questions about each caregiver's experience with disabled children, as well as what they can do to accommodate your child's special needs. And, of course, you want a nanny that will focus on your child as a person, rather than on their disabilities.

We recognize that caring for a special needs child is often a team approach, and we ask parents to be honest and up-front about their child's abilities and limitations. Their nanny should know about daily routines, including any physical or occupational therapies, medication schedules, doctors' appointments, and so forth.

Parents should give the nanny any testing equipment, medicines, or special equipment that the child needs, and teach the nanny how to use them. They should also explain if the nanny will be responsible for regular procedures, such as finger prick tests to check blood sugar levels. Let the nanny know if your child needs help putting on, taking off, or using braces, artificial limbs, or other equipment. Teach the nanny about your child's seeing-eye dog or other type of service animal. And explain if your child needs special medications, such as a shot in case of an allergic reaction. If your child is prone to seizures, be clear about the protocol during these episodes.

Before hiring a nanny, ask if she's ever dealt with an emergency or special needs situation. If so, what was the situation and how was it handled? Be sure to familiarize your nanny with your family's emergency procedures, and provide her with a list of the medical personnel that cares for your child in an emergency.

Your special needs child should have a competent, patient, and nurturing nanny caring for them. And you should have open, honest communication with the nanny to assess how your child is doing. In an ideal situation, the nanny will support your efforts to help your special needs child thrive.

In our survey the respondents reported working with children that had special needs such as autism, down syndrome, attention deficit disorder (ADD) and cerebral palsy, to name a few conditions. As you search for a nanny to care for your special needs child, you may want to consider a nanny with experience or special training in this area. Your local community may be able to provide training for your nanny that is specific to your needs.

## Emergency Preparedness – Important for All Children

It is important to take the lead and make sure that your nanny is equipped to handle emergencies in your home. All nannies should be certified in infant CPR if appropriate to your situation and child CPR for older children. If your nanny comes in without this education, you should include the training as condition of employment. The American Red Cross (www.redcross.org) provides this type of training and can help you locate training in your area.

Beyond CPR, and depending on where your live, your nanny should be prepared for and understand the actions to take in the event of a natural disaster. If you live in hurricane, tornado or earthquake country, there should be a family master plan in the event of an emergency. All families should have a fire escape plan and a safe place to meet up once the crisis is over. Don't expect your nanny to know what to do, be sure she is prepared to meet emergencies in a calm and responsible manner.

**Emergency Contacts**

You should maintain an emergency contact list: one copy should be kept in the home, and the other copy should be kept with the nanny at all times. Here is a starter list to help you build a comprehensive emergency contact list:

- Parents' home, work, and cell phone numbers

- Parents' work addresses

- Parents' car license plate numbers

- Neighbors' home and cell phone numbers

- Close (physically) relatives' home, work, and cell numbers

- Poison Control Center

- 911 in your area

- Local sheriff, police and fire house numbers — make sure your nanny knows the 911 procedures for cell phones and digital (Internet) land line numbers, not hooked into the 911 system

- You should have one land line not using electricity with a traditional hand set (not a mobile line)

- Your pediatrician, dentist, and veterinarian's number, if you have pets

- The local hospital as a last resort

You should also have a prepared emergency kit appropriate for the size of your family plus your nanny.

# The Life of a Family

Whether you are the parent of a child with special needs, a family with two working parents, parents of the same sex, or a single parent, every family is special. Your nanny becomes an important member of your team, and we encourage you to consider your nanny as an extension of yourself. The most important aspect of life to which a nanny can contribute is free time to spend with your child. Each family will have a different combination of activities, but all families will share the following experiences from time to time and need to designate who will be responsible for certain activities. By using your time for quality interaction with your child and having your nanny handle some routine activities, your family will benefit in the long run.

- **Transportation:** Driving your child to doctor's appointments, dentist appointments, sporting activities—practices, games, etc.

- **Social activities:** Birthday parties for your child's friends, visits with extended family, Gymboree®, swimming lessons, music lessons, dance lessons, play dates, sports activities, physical therapy, trips to the park, etc.

- **School work:** Homework, study skills, tutoring, advanced classes, homeschooling

- **Exercise:** Formal exercise programs, outdoor play activities

- **Errands:** For the child and for the family

- **Chores:** Preparing meals, cleaning the kitchen, laundry

In our survey from 2009 and 2010 with nannies and babysitters, 74% (N=2,527) of the respondents are helping out with more than just childcare. While the majority of nannies and babysitters focus on the needs of the children in their care, it is not unusual for them to help around the house.

**QUESTION: ARE YOU EXPECTED TO PERFORM
DUTIES OTHER THAN CHILD CARE?**

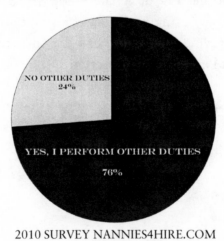

NO OTHER DUTIES
24%

YES, I PERFORM OTHER DUTIES
76%

2010 SURVEY NANNIES4HIRE.COM

Here is the breakdown of 2,255 nannies and babysitters:

| | | |
|---|---|---|
| Housekeeping | Child only | 59% |
| Housekeeping | Family | 34% |
| Meal Preparation | Child only | 77% |
| Meal Preparation | Family | 20% |
| Errands | Child only | 44% |
| Errands | Family | 31% |
| Dishes | Child only | 55% |
| Dishes | Family | 45% |
| Child only activities | | 77% |
| Family activities | | 19% |

Is there a difference between the additional work being performed by full-time and part-time caregivers? Here is how our survey breaks down:

| | | | | | |
|---|---|---|---|---|---|
| Housekeeping | Child only | Full-time | 62% | Part-time | 55% |
| Housekeeping | Family | Full-time | 35% | Part-time | 31% |
| Meal Preparation | Child only | Full-time | 77% | Part-time | 79% |
| Meal Preparation | Family | Full-time | 24% | Part-time | 15% |
| Errands | Child only | Full-time | 45% | Part-time | 35% |
| Errands | Family | Full-time | 62% | Part-time | 23% |
| Dishes | Child only | Full-time | 55% | Part-time | 54% |
| Dishes | Family | Full-time | 48% | Part-time | 37% |

Today's caregivers are very likely to help you around the house. The important thing to remember is that time to do the chores must be factored into the day, so your child is not neglected.

nine

# So How Much Will All This Cost Me?

Your nanny's hourly wage or salary is a combination of a number of factors: experience, education, duties, and hours. You will also consider living expenses such as room and board if you have a live-in nanny and the number of children in the nanny's care. So that you can get an idea of the compensation today's nannies are receiving, let's look at the breakdown in our survey of nannies and babysitters.

| HOURLY WAGES FOR NANNIES AND BABYSITTERS, FULL-TIME VS. PART-TIME | | |
|---|---|---|
| | **Full-time** | **Part-Time** |
| $6 or less | 7% | 4% |
| $7-8 | 8% | 6% |
| $9-$10 | 16% | 19% |
| $11-$12 | 17% | 24% |
| $13-$15 | 26% | 29% |

| HOURLY WAGES FOR NANNIES AND BABYSITTERS, FULL-TIME VS. PART-TIME | | |
|---|---|---|
| | **Full-time** | **Part-Time** |
| $16 | 6% | 5% |
| $17 | 3% | 2% |
| $18 | 4% | 3% |
| $19 | 1% | .03% |
| $20 | 5% | 4% |
| $21-25 | 3% | 3% |
| Over $25 | 1% | 1% |

## Factors that Make a Difference in Wages

The biggest factor in determining the rate of pay for your full-time nanny and babysitter is experience. Those caregivers with one year of experience earned an average hourly wage of $9 to $10 while those with over 5 years of experience earned an average of $13 to $15. In addition to wages, how the caregiver views their occupation is also a factor of experience. Seventy percent of respondents with 10 or more years' experience referred to their occupation as a nanny, compared with 30% with 10 or more years' experience who called themselves babysitters.

The number of children in the family does not influence wages as much as one might think. Most caregivers who replied to our survey are taking care of two children, ages 3-5, on a full-time basis. Less experienced caregivers attending to more than five children did not earn what a more experienced caregiver earns when caring for only two children ages 3-5.

Where you live may have an impact on your budget. Those caregivers who live in a city are earning $13 to $15 per hour as a babysitter (25%) while those in the suburbs and rural areas are earning $9 to $10 per hour. Those caregivers who see themselves as a nanny earned on average $13 to $15 per hour regardless of where they lived.

# Communication, the Key to Success

Like most relationships, communication between the parties involved has a great deal to do with the success or failure of the partnership. It is no different between you and your nanny. How much communication you need on a daily basis really has to do with your personal preferences. You want to create a communication structure that provides you with an understanding of your child's day so you won't miss any important milestones or the daily experiences of your child.

There is no right or wrong to your communication structure. What is important here is that it works for you. There will be some families that will, no matter what, have a weekly meeting. The meeting is scheduled each week, and the nanny knows to keep a journal or notes of things that happen throughout the week. Problems, questions, scheduling requests, and the business of being a nanny are discussed in the weekly meeting. Some families will just have a brief updating discussion every day.

Some nannies like to keep a daily journal and will jot everything down that happens throughout the day. The parents can then just flip to the notebook and see what happened that day. This is very common when it comes to babies. A nanny will document: how many ounces of formula or bottled milk that the baby took, how many diapers were soiled, how the stools were, what the baby did, and document every other situation. This is also a wonderful way to make recommendations to the parents as well as keep them informed about the health of the child. For example, if a child is on medication, the nanny can write down, "This is the time they took the medication; here is what they took." A daily notebook goes a long way for a parent's peace of mind.

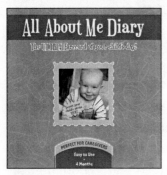

There are many commercial nanny journals on the market today, and you will want to find one that meets your needs. The *All About Me Diary* [4] by Joan Ahlers and Cheryl Tallman is designed for infants and provides trigger questions to help the nanny cover the many things throughout the day.

Here is an example of a journal page:

Date _Sept 30_

FEEDINGS:

| Time | Solids | | Liquids |
|---|---|---|---|
| 7:30 | Breakfast: | Pears, Peaches, Oatmeal | breastfed |
| 10:00 | Snack: | ½ banana, | 4 oz. breastmilk |
| 12:20 | Lunch: | Sweet potatoes, Peas, Apples | water |
| 3:30 | Snack: | | 5 oz breastmilk |
| 6:30 | Dinner: | Cauliflower, Broccoli, Mangos | breastfed |

B.M.'s:   No ___   Yes _X_   How Many? _2_

NAPS:                              MEDICATIONS:

| Sleep | Wake | Which? | | Time |
|---|---|---|---|---|
| 11:10 | 12:10 | none | | : |
| 3:45 | 5:00 | | | : |
| : | : | | | : |
| : | : | | | : |

ACTIVITIES: walk in the park, blocks, music, reading nursery rhymes

COMMENTS: Lots of smiles today!

* running low on wipes

---

4  All About Me Diary - Available at www.Freshbaby.com

While a formal journal is a nice keepsake, it is not necessary as children get older. A spiral notebook will work just as well. It is important for you to share with your nanny what you would like to know about your child everyday. Remember, the nanny is an extension of yourself, so be sure to share all the information about your child that you are interested in tracking. Many families document diet and exercise, TV and computer use, moods, questions the child may have, and reminders about school and social activities coming up in the week.

## Business Meetings – Employee and Management

One of the keys to successful communication is the separation of business from family life. Your nanny is responsible for communicating the day-to-day aspects of your child's life in the format that works for you. It is your responsibility to provide a format for your nanny to discuss aspects of your child's growth and development that you want to follow. It is also your responsibility to provide a forum for your nanny to discuss her employment situation. Asking for time off, changing schedules, and performance evaluations should be discussed at a set time and place. A good time to check in on the business aspect of your relationship could be a fifteen minute conversation when you give your nanny her paycheck on a weekly or bi-weekly basis. This way, the emotions of the day, on both sides, don't influence the communication.

## Performance Evaluations

The first year with a new nanny provides the opportunity to structure time to give feedback in a productive way. A three part approach to discussing performance will help you keep your lines of communication open. It is often referred to as a feedback sandwich, especially if there is a negative behavior or action that you need to discuss. By providing positive feedback first, your nanny will be able to relax and then hear your concerns without being defensive. After you have delivered any negative information, make sure you close your discussion with more positive feedback. It is the situation that you wish to change, not your relationships.

One approach to hiring a new nanny is to utilize an introductory period of three months. A temporary three month contract helps you spell out your employment expectations in a formal and legal manner. It is appropriate to have a given wage or salary during the introductory period, with a raise in pay at the end of the three month period. Your nanny has something to look forward to and you are going to receive the level of service that you are expecting. In addition, the three months puts both you and your nanny on notice that this is a trial to see if the match is right for your nanny and your family. During this time, you will want to have regularly scheduled meetings on how things are going. Of course, you will always want to leave your door open to discuss emergencies or problems when they come up, not two weeks later. It is very important for you to provide positive feedback to your nanny on an ongoing basis. It is a challenging job to deal with a child 40 hours a week, and the child is not going to tell the nanny if she is doing a good or poor job. That is up to you. We recommend the following performance evaluation schedule to keep things running smoothly:

- **Two weeks:** This initial meeting provides you both with the opportunity to clarify communications, discuss what's working and not working, and any changes you would like to see made. This is also a good time to check in with your child, if the child is old enough, to see how they like spending time with the nanny. Listen carefully: children will tell you the truth about their feelings.

- **One month:** By this time, you should have a well established routine in your household. Any corrective measures should have been communicated as they occurred. It is a good time to ask your nanny if she has any questions, challenges, or issues she would like to discuss with you.

- **Two months:** This is the time to evaluate if you are happy with your nanny's performance. If you are, it is a good time to praise the job your nanny is doing. If you are not happy, it is the time to give your nanny 30 days' notice or severance pay with the understanding you will not be renewing the contract once the introductory period is concluded.

- **Three months:** You are now entering into a long-term relationship with your nanny. By now, you both know much more about each other than when the relationship first began, and it is time to amend your contract to reflect any changes. The honeymoon is over, and both of you are operating at your normal pace and way of living. Reward good performance with an incremental wage or salary raise and set a time in a year for another performance evaluation.

# Get It in Writing

There are many benefits to having a contract with your nanny. The most important distinction is that it is not possible to remember all the details of spoken conversations over time. Also, what you say may not be what your nanny hears. A contract is a way to document those items in your relationship like wage or salary, hours, confidentiality, details of your work assignment, transportation, days off, vacation and benefits. In Chapter Eight we discussed some of the responsibilities of a nanny, which you may want to include in your contract. Here are some of the basic clauses in a contract and what they mean to your family.

## Confidentiality and Your Nanny Contract

Most nanny contracts have a confidentiality clause stating that your nanny will not repeat anything heard or seen within the home, unless the nanny is concerned about possible abuse issues. A confidentiality clause protects the family from having the nanny repeat private information about you to others. Obviously, this is also a matter of professionalism and common courtesy, but having your nanny sign a contract with a confidentiality clause helps you have some peace of mind that your nanny will not tell friends or family how much money the family makes or any other personal issues that may arise. Signing a contract with a confidentiality clause doesn't mean that you find your nanny untrustworthy, which is something you might have to explain to your nanny. It simply means that you are protecting your family, just in case!

## What Should Be in Your Nanny Contract?

If you are signing a nanny contract with your nanny, make sure that the following is directly stated within the contract so that there is no confusion at a later date:

- The nanny contract must have all of the responsibilities that the nanny will be held accountable for. This includes taking care of your child, specific household chores, and any educational or social activities the nanny will be in charge of.

- Your nanny work agreement must have the wage or salary in it, along with the dates that the nanny will be receiving her paychecks. It should also provide information about any employment benefits, i.e., health insurance and paid time off, and tax information that is applicable.

- Nanny contracts should also include, if appropriate, if the nanny is expected to watch your child overnight, how often, when, etc., and if the nanny is expected to watch your child on trips.

- It should also include the nanny's days off, the days the nanny is expected to work, the hours the nanny is expected to work, and the details of any overtime compensation that may be due for time worked beyond 40 hours a week.

- If you are providing the nanny's transportation, an agreement about gas and use of the car should be included in the contract.

- Finally, the nanny contract should include the nanny's hire date, the date that the contract is expected to expire, the contractually permitted reasons for ending the employment relationship before the contract expires, and the terms of any cash or benefits that may be due the nanny upon her separation from employment.

As you can see, there is a lot of information that is included in a nanny contract. By talking to your nanny and adding her input, you can create a detailed contract. See the Appendix for a copy of a contract.

## What Happens If the Contract Is Broken?

It is best not to break the signed nanny contract. However, if there is a circumstance that arises in which you feel you or your nanny must break the agreement, then the contract should also detail what would happen should the contract be broken. Most contracts will require that your nanny gives two weeks' notice if she plans on quitting. It gives the family a little time to find back-up childcare and tie up any loose ends.

Although a nanny contract isn't usually a legally binding contract, it is a professional agreement between the nanny and the employer.

## Where to Get a Nanny Contract

As the employer, you should take the lead on providing a nanny contract. One great resource to look for a nanny contract is on the Internet. By seeing a variety of sample contracts, you will quickly see what you need in your agreement. Most of the time, these nanny contracts are offered for free on the Internet, but you may have to register with the website. There is a sample contract available to registered members at Nannies4hire.com and in the Appendix.

If you are working with a nanny agency, the nanny contract will most often be handled through the agency. The agency will have both the nanny and the family sign the agreement.

Finding a nanny contract isn't hard to do, but it is important to have for both parties involved! Once you have printed a nanny contract and have agreed to it, it needs to be signed by everyone involved, and everyone must keep a copy of the contract for his or her file.

## Who Writes the Nanny Contract?

Many nannies are given a contract which has been drawn up beforehand by the employer. However, it isn't completely inappropriate to ask to write the contract or fill it out together, rather than having one done ahead of time.

A nanny should be allowed to look over the contract in detail and be given some time to discuss it with you, as the employer, or even a trusted advisor who can determine if the contract is appropriate and offer any advice before the nanny signs it.

As the employer, be open to discussion if your nanny finds something within the contract that she may have a concern about. Being upfront from the get-go creates an open line of communication on both sides, which makes the nanny experience a positive one!

### Do As We Say – Not As We Do –  The Facts about Nanny Contracts

A nanny contract is the only document that can help restore peace in the event of a misunderstanding. In our survey of working nannies, the majority of nannies do not have a contract, which is clearly a disadvantage for both parties. Of the 737 responses from nannies, only 178 (24%) had a contract compared to 508 (76%) who did not have a contract. The chart below demonstrates the impact of this decision.

QUESTION: DO YOU  HAVE A SIGNED CONTRACT?

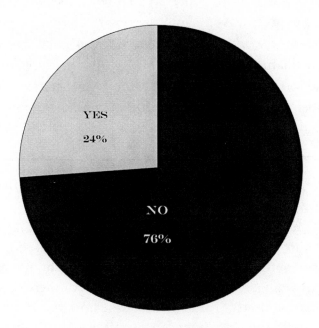

2010 Survey NANNIES4HIRE.COM

## Why Use a Nanny Contract?

Nanny employment contracts show that both the employer and the nanny are taking their work agreement very seriously.

An employer asking a nanny to sign a contract helps ensure that the nanny sees herself as a professional and, in most cases, will then act as a professional. It also helps you both get clear on what is expected of you, as an employer. For the nanny, it helps her know what her pay and benefits will be as well as your expectations of her work performance.

Having a nanny contract also helps alleviate nanny turnover because all of the expectations are spelled out in a contract. A nanny or an employer can't say that he or she wasn't aware of what was expected. As a nanny, if you are unsatisfied with some aspect of your working conditions, you can point to the agreement, not blame the person. A nanny and an employer can go back and forth with expectations before a final contract is signed. Remember, this is a two-way street that benefits your child in the long run.

### Candi's Take on Benefits for Your Nanny

You are excited about the prospect of hiring a nanny to help take care of your child, but you're not sure what types of benefits you should be providing. Adding to your challenge, there's no hard-and-fast "rules" that outline how you should handle this situation. Wages/salaries and benefits vary depending on:

- The nanny's experience,
- Her responsibilities,

- The number of hours needed,
- Whether she lives-in or lives-out,
- Your geographic location — nannies in big cities typically earn more than nannies in small towns,

Other guidelines to keep in mind:

- Determine an hourly rate that you're willing to pay, and discuss the wage and responsibilities with your nanny up-front,
- Be prepared to pay overtime for nannies that work more than a certain number of hours per week — under the Fair Labor Standards Act (FLSA), 40 hours is a standard workweek in most states. A live-out nanny should be paid 1.5 times their hourly pay for overtime hours. But state labor laws can grant more overtime eligibility than the FLSA. In California, for example, standard pay is based on an eight-hour day, instead of a 40 hour work week, so if your nanny works a 10-hour day, you'd need to pay her two hours of overtime, even if her weekly hours don't exceed 40. There are other exceptions for live-in, salaried employees. Good resources for more specifics are www.DOL.gov and www.GTM.com,
- Nannies will expect to be paid weekly, bi-weekly or monthly. Some states have laws that govern the frequency with which employees must be paid,
- Paid time off, vacation, and sick leave typically accumulate over time. Some families require that a nanny work for a certain amount of time

(usually two to three months) before they offer paid time off. Two paid weeks off per year is standard after the nanny has been employed for a determined amount of time,

- Families who hire live-in nannies may offer a car for the nanny's exclusive use,
- Many families will travel, take their nanny along, and agree to pay their travel expenses. The nanny is usually responsible for some childcare while traveling but will also be allowed to enjoy the vacation as well,
- Many families offer paid holidays for New Year's Day, Memorial Day, July 4th, Labor Day, Thanksgiving, Christmas and New Year's Eve,
- Providing medical insurance can be negotiated between the family and the nanny. Some families will pay the entire policy while others may pay a certain dollar amount. Negotiate that with your nanny if that is a benefit you want to provide,
- Bonuses are always appreciated. If your nanny is doing an exceptional job, consider rewarding her with a financial bonus, either at the holidays, during the year "just because" or if she will be extending her commitment with your family.

*Section Three*
# Down to Basics, Finding Your Nanny

twelve

# Finding Your Nanny

The rapid integration of technology in our lives should make finding a high quality caregiver as easy as clicking a mouse. If you use a high-quality database service, such as Nannies4hire. com or Care4hire.com, you know there is a well established business with an exemplary reputation behind you. If you use online services that are just a listing or electronic classified ad, you will want to be very careful of the buyer-beware approach to the care of your child. Experience with the process of hiring and understanding the needs of your family is an important factor when deciding your source for nanny candidates. If you are new to the process, you may want to go with an experienced and reliable source which can provide answers to your questions.

No matter what the source, you are the one responsible for the ultimate decision, so you'll want to use all the resources at your disposal to make a good choice. Here are the sources commonly used to locate a nanny in your community:

**Word of Mouth:** Finding a nanny through word of mouth, like all sources, has its pros and cons. You may end up with the child of a friend who is between jobs. Getting a referral on an organization or service that helped your friends find a great nanny is a better resource for you.

**Classified Ads:** Your local newspaper, church bulletin, or local college are traditional mediums for advertising for childcare help. Since the people who will see your ad are looking for work, you may be opening yourself up to a group of people not necessarily in the business of child care. Some people make the mistake of thinking that caring for children is easy work. You will have to double check references and do local and national background checks and careful interviews to weed out the I'll-take-anything job seekers and to find those seriously pursuing a career in childcare.

**Online Classified Ads:** An online classified advertisement is a generic free or low cost listing. These lists can be viewed by anyone and are not protected by passwords or supervised by the listing service as are the ads through a reputable site, like Nannies4hire.com, where your personal information cannot be seen by the public. Online classified ads are wide open with the ease of access and the competitive nature of the Internet. You will discover a huge number of sites offering to host your ad for a nanny for free or a small fee. Many free services make their money through ads and by other not-so-transparent means, like installing ads on your computer or tracking your computer usage. Good virus tracking or anti-spyware software can remove these uninvited guests from your computer. Remember that once you enter your personal information in a public environment, your phone and email address is there for all to see. Even after you take your ad down, electronic data lives on in cache systems with no guarantees of removal. Another danger of electronic ads is that you are telling the world that you have a child in your home, something you would not want predators, such as pedophiles, to know. If your phone number is listed in the telephone directory of your phone company, their online directory service not only lists your address on the Internet, it provides a map to where you live. To remove this feature, you must call your phone company and ask them to remove your street address from the listing. If you go with a free ad service, make sure you know the reputation of the provider.

**Nanny Placement Services:** There are agencies which will do all of the work for you for a fee, which can range from $800 to $5,000 [5]or more. This type of service should provide you with a nanny candidate that has been through a criminal and child-abuse background check, verification of previous education and employment records, current references that have been verified, verification of CPR training, and child care training, if appropriate. Another way to look at this is that the agency is doing the work for you, and you want to make sure it has an excellent reputation for follow-through. You should also have in writing an agreement about getting a refund or replacement nanny should the nanny you hire not work out.

**Online Nanny Database Service:** With today's technology, online database services are the best of all worlds. They provide you with data on available nannies and caregivers in your local area by providing a search by zip code and help you identify good candidates by your priorities. For example, the services provided by Nannies4hire.com and Care4hire. com give you a snapshot view of available candidates at no charge. Here is an example of the information from the free search:

---

5 International Nanny Association website, www.nanny.org

## Melissa
## Nanny ID# 411753

### *Basic Information*

**First Name:**    Melissa
**Gender:**        female
**Age:**           22
**Location:**      Sacramento, CA 94204

**Contact Information**

To view, Please    Login    or    Register

**Background Information:**
**Have you ever been arrested or convicted of any offense?**    No

**Family Information**
**Do you have children:**    No

**If your children will accompany you, please list their ages:**

**Citizenship Information**

**Nationality:**              American
**Country of Origin:**        US

**Health Information**

**Weight:**    135
**Height:**    5'9"
**Do you smoke?**    No

**Are you currently under any doctor's care, receiving counseling or have any physical, mental or medical impairments, which would interfere with your ability to perform the job?**    No

### *Skills Information*

**What is your level of education?** College Degree
**Languages**                        English
**Do you have a valid driver's license?**    Yes
**Can you swim?**                    Yes

## *Employment Information*

**Preferred Weekly Salary:** 0-100, 100-200, 200-300, 300-400, 400-500, 500-600, 600-700, 700-800+

**Position Duration:** Permanent/Full-Time

**When are you available to start?:** Start Date is Flexible

**You would prefer to live:** Live-in

**Preferred States:** CA, CO, FL, HI, MN, NJ, PA, TX, DC

**You would be willing to care for the following ages:** I would prefer to provide care for ages infant to 12 with family sizes up to 5

**Nanny Experience:** 3 years of experience caring for ages Infant to 12 with family sizes up to 5

**Babysitting Experience:** 10+ years of experience caring for ages Infant to 12 with family sizes up to 5

**You can care for the elderly:** Yes

**Elder/Companion Care Experience:** When attending High School, I volunteered in a Nursing Home in my community. I would play cards with the residents and just be available to chat and be a companion to them.

**Available for special needs:** Disabilities, Behavioral Issues, Twins/Multiples

**Do you have a car to bring to the job?** Yes

## *Availability Information*

| | Mon | Tues | Wed | Thurs | Fri | Sat | Sun |
|---|:---:|:---:|:---:|:---:|:---:|:---:|:---:|
| Early Morning (6a-9a) | ✓ | ✓ | ✓ | ✓ | ✓ | ✓ | ✓ |
| Late Morning (9a-12p) | ✓ | ✓ | ✓ | ✓ | ✓ | ✓ | ✓ |
| Early Afternoon (12p-3p) | ✓ | ✓ | ✓ | ✓ | ✓ | ✓ | ✓ |
| Late Afternoon (3p-6p) | ✓ | ✓ | ✓ | ✓ | ✓ | ✓ | ✓ |
| Early Evening (6p-9p) | ✓ | ✓ | ✓ | ✓ | ✓ | ✓ | ✓ |
| Late Evening (9-12) | ✓ | ✓ | ✓ | ✓ | ✓ | ✓ | ✓ |
| Overnight (12a-6a) | ✓ | ✓ | ✓ | ✓ | ✓ | ✓ | ✓ |

## Why do you want to become a nanny?

I LOVE CHILDREN! I love to see their smiling faces and I love to see them grow into young adults. Children are amazing and are our future.

## Describe your past childcare experience:

I have been involved in childcare since I was 15 years old. I started out babysitting for families in my neighborhood and eventually branched out to families all over my town. I cared for children infant to 12 years old; caring for up to 5 children at a time. I was also a lifeguard at my local pool during the summer. During College I enjoyed nannying for a family of 4. The children were 7, 5, 3 & 1 when I started. I was responsible for childcare, light housekeeping, transporting the children, meal preparation, children's laundry and we loved going to the zoo, park, museum, etc. I love seeing them grow. I still am considered part of their family. Besides my nanny experience, I also helped out in a daycare setting. I helped mostly in the infant room and enjoyed every minute of it. I am a college graduate with a degree in Elementary Education. I love teaching, but want to work 1 on 1 with children and use my knowledge to help the little ones prepare for school.

## Additional Comments:

I am so excited about this opportunity and can't wait to get to know your family. I want you to feel comfortable leaving the home and know your children are in good hands.

Fees are based on the level of service desired. For example, Nannies4hire.com offers three levels of service: Premier, which includes 99 days of job posting, database access and comprehensive background checks; Platinum, which includes 60 days of job posting, database access and a state-wide criminal history search; and Gold, which provides 30 days of job posting and database access. You decide which level of service meets your needs. To see the current rates, please visit Nannies4hire.com.

Regardless of the method you choose to find your nanny, make sure that you are using a reliable source. What makes a source reliable? It is all a matter of trust. Does the company offer customer service if you have an issue? Can the company help you navigate the many legal and tax issues that come from hiring household help? Do they offer you the resources you need to make a good decision? It is important to have a resource you can depend on as you choose the person to care for your child.

# The Interview Process

Now that you have chosen the nanny candidates that are of interest to you, you have a few options for narrowing your choices. The first option is to thoroughly interview your nanny candidates. There are several ways in which you can conduct your interviews. Here are some suggestions to make the process easier for you:

1. Prepare an interview schedule for phone interviews. Estimate 15-30 minutes per call.

2. Prepare your initial screening questions. These questions are designed to eliminate candidates from your pool based on specific information, such as availability for your schedule, identifying conflicts with other commitments, and meeting your transportation and experience requirements.

3. Prepare an in-person interview schedule for the screening interview. These interviews should last between 30 and 60 minutes and should not include your child. Once you have decided on your final two or three candidates, verified their references, and

performed their background checks, you can schedule the selection interviews that will include your child.

## Email Invitation for an Interview

If you are conducting your search using online tools and agencies, email may be the easiest and most efficient way of inviting candidates to an interview. Start the process by exchanging information via email or phone about your nanny position and the interest level of the nanny. After you have determined you would like to meet the candidate in person, schedule an interview. Because of the large amounts of spam and unwanted email people receive these days, make sure your email subject line is specific. You might use, "Phone Interview for Nanny Opening." In the body of the message, give your nanny candidates two or three interview times to choose from and an estimate of how long to set aside for the interview. Make sure you include the best possible way to reach you, whether it is by email or phone.

## Step One: The Phone Interview

This type of interview is designed for convenience, but it should be conducted using the proper etiquette of an interview. Be aware if your nanny candidate is speaking to you from a quiet area and using the language and manners appropriate for an interview. At the end of the interview, let the nanny candidate know what they can expect. For example, you can let the candidate know that you will be following up with an email or a phone call about the next steps. Even if you reject the candidate, thank them for their time and let them know you are going to be interviewing other candidates. Here is some suggested language for a follow-up email:

*Thank you for your time and your interest in the nanny position. We had many candidates for the position, and we regret we will not be able to offer you employment at this time. Good luck in your job search; we wish you the best.*

## Step Two: The In-Person Interview

Once you have decided which candidates you wish to meet in person, you will choose the location of the interview based on your own personal preferences. If your privacy is very important, you may want to meet in a neutral location, such as a coffee house. You should expect the nanny candidates to be well groomed, punctual, and using good manners. The face-to-face interview is important to see how you feel with the candidates as well as to see a small window into how they will relate to your child. Are the candidates friendly, inquisitive, and interested in knowing more about your child than the salary?

At this time, it is important to explain your expectations and your job requirements in detail. You'll want to get references, request school documentation if it is important to you, and ask about any special needs or circumstances the candidate may have. Here are some common questions:

- What do you like about caring for children in their home?

- Why did you leave your last position?

- What aspects of the job do you like the best? The least?

- How long have you been a nanny?

- Have you taken any childcare classes?

- What ages were the children you have cared for?

- Tell me about your family life.

- Did you ever have a nanny as a child? How was that experience for you?

- What do you think children like best about you?

- Have you ever experienced an emergency while caring for children?

- How do you think you would handle an emergency?

- Do you drive? How is your driving record?

- Explore what geographic areas the candidate has lived in. This will be important for the background checks.

- What kind of activities will you do with children this age?

- How do you handle problems that arise behaviorally and emotionally with a child this age?

- What is the most important aspect of a nanny position?

- Can you tell me how you would handle getting a child ready for school, such as feeding, dressing, etc. and getting them to school on time?

- When would you call 911? When would you simply call the doctor?

- Do you cook? Will you do some house cleaning?

- Would you be willing to attend more child development classes?

- Have you been trained in infant/child CPR? Would you be willing to take the training?

- How do you discipline a child who is acting out or not following your instructions?

- Do you prefer to work with children of a certain age? Do you prefer working with boys or girls?

- Are you a smoker? Do you follow a particular eating plan?

- Have you ever had problems with the parents of children you cared for?

- What are some ways you would spend the day with my child?

## Six Legal Questions You Can Ask A Nanny Candidate

When you're interviewing a nanny candidate, you should be aware that some questions are legal and some are not. It's always important to maintain a level of professionalism as you're interviewing candidates. Read on to find out what legal questions you can ask a nanny candidate.

1. You can ask what a nanny's full name is.

2. You can ask if she has any criminal convictions.

3. You can ask if she has any felony charges pending against her.

4. You can ask if a nanny is over the age of 18.

5. You can ask how long she has lived in her current residence.

6. You can ask if the nanny candidate is legally authorized to work in the United States and/or Canada.

Before the interviews end, make sure you ask the candidates to sign a release form giving you permission to check their references and background. Without a signed release, you are limited in the information you can obtain about your candidates. Asking detailed questions of former employers and references provides you with insight into the character of the candidate.

## Step Three: Checking References

When you have decided on your final candidates, it is important to check the references and perform a background search. Although this is a time-consuming part of the interview process, it is essential because people tend to put their best foot forward during an interview. Sometimes, people will give you more information by what they don't say, rather than what they do say. If an answer is non-specific or vague, you may want to eliminate this candidate. It is also a good idea to see if the person would re-hire the candidate. You'll be able to tell by their tone if the candidate is a person you want working for you. It is also important to ask for a land line to check the references. You will be able to verify the ownership of the phone and if it is actually at the home. Cell phones, while convenient, are not as easy to verify.

Inform your candidates that you will be doing a background check and other verifications on them. These include:

**Character references** – Find out personality traits about the applicant, such as if she's warm and loving around children and whether she's organized and punctual.

**Drug testing** – Drug testing is a way to make sure that an applicant does not have illegal substances in her system.

**Higher education verification** – If you're looking for a nanny with college credentials, you can check to see whether the information she's given you is accurate.

**Sex offender/child abuse registry** – You can verify whether an applicant has a criminal record involving children.

When searching for a nanny, it is critical for the safety of all involved to run thorough background checks. Families assume responsibility for all background verification of a nanny candidate. Listed below are some other background checks you may obtain:

- Driving Records

- Social Security Number Trace

- Past Employment Verification

- Criminal Records

## Avoiding Illegal Questions

When conducting an interview, make sure you don't ask illegal questions of a nanny candidate. It's always best to keep the questions focused on items that relate to the candidate's role as a nanny and how she will perform her job duties. The following is a list of illegal questions you don't want to ask a nanny during an interview.

- Don't ask your nanny what her maiden name was.

- Don't ask your nanny if she has ever been arrested.

However, you can ask if she has been convicted of a crime or has felony charges pending against her.

- Don't ask your nanny what year she was born.

- Don't ask your nanny what country she has citizenship with. However, you can ask if she is legally authorized to work in the United States and/or Canada.

## What You Can Get From A Nanny Background Check

When you decide to do a nanny background check, you can learn a great deal of information about a candidate. If you're not sure what you should bother checking or what you'll learn with nanny background checks, this guide will fill you in on the basics.

**Criminal Record**- You'll want to make sure your nanny doesn't have any offenses on her criminal record that would make you uneasy about having her watching your child.

**Driving Record** – The driving record check will fill you in on a nanny's level of responsibility. You'll learn things like whether there have been any alcohol or drug-related incidents, as well as a nanny's driving history.

**Employment** – During the nanny background check, you will want to verify your nanny's previous employment. This will verify the amount of experience that she has as well as how accurate the dates are that she's given you.

**Social Security** – Checking your nanny's Social Security information verifies that the number belongs to her and where she is living now or where she has lived previously.

**Why It's Important to Do the Background Check**

Although it can be tempting to hire the first nanny you come across who meets all the qualifications you're looking for, it is definitely a smart decision to do a background check. Although you usually won't find anything that should deter you from hiring a nanny candidate, it's always better to err on the side of caution. The nanny background check can reveal information you wouldn't otherwise be privy to.

For example, take the case of a California nanny who had a fatal accident in 2003. A family in a different state hired her from an advertisement and neglected to do a background check. Had they done a background check of the nanny's driving record, they would have found that the woman had her driver's license suspended twice for a high blood-alcohol level and that she had been involved in a fatal accident. Such a marked driving record would be an instant red flag against hiring that nanny.

**Step 4: The Real Test - Having the Nanny Candidates Meet Your Child**

There is one last step before you offer the position to your best nanny candidate: introducing her to your child. Depending on the age of your child, you will want to design the schedule to meet your child's needs. Set aside a few hours for your nanny candidates to spend time alone with your child. On the first visit, you can remain in the house and, to allow one-on-one interaction, you will want to go to another room. Children may not feel comfortable at first with a new person, so getting your child to interact with the prospective nanny is a plus.

On the next day, leave your child with the nanny candidates, one-on-one, for a brief trial run. Stop by the house unannounced before you are expected. Observe the candidates' reaction, if there is any. Spend time now with your child and the candidates so you can observe their interactions first-hand. Do the nanny candidates create fun activities for your child? Do they act with professionalism when you are in and out of your home? While it is appropriate to check with your child and see if they enjoyed their time with the nanny candidates, your child does not share your priorities. Knowing that your child is happy, safe and well mannered is the goal.

When you are comfortable with choosing the right nanny candidate for your family, you are ready to make her an offer and life with your new nanny begins.

*Section Four*

# After the Honeymoon: What to Expect from Your Nanny

# Your Working Relationship

As in any new job, your nanny wants to make a good impression and meet your expectations. That is why it is important for the two of you to create a game plan that you both understand and agree upon. Conversations tend to disappear or change over time, so if an issue is important to you, make sure you write it down. It is also important to train your nanny to write things down from her very first day.

From day one, you and your nanny are on a team to care for, nurture, educate and groom your child to be a happy and healthy adult. When we asked our nannies and babysitters if they felt appreciated in our survey of 2010, the overall response was YES!

The nannies were asked what made them feel appreciated and the response was very simple but important, being thanked each day for their work with their charges. More importantly, they valued being thanked for a specific action, like, "Thank you for helping Sam with his math homework. He was really stuck on that problem, and you helped him to understand it."

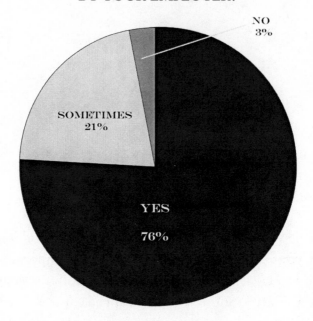

QUESTION: DO YOU FEEL APPRECIATED
BY YOUR EMPLOYER?

NO
3%

SOMETIMES
21%

YES

76%

2010 SURVEY NANNIES4HIRE.COM

Nannies also feel appreciated when parents respect them in front of the children, keep their word about being home on time, call if there will be a delay, honor the nanny's special requests, such as the need to make a doctor's appointment, and teach their children to say thank you to the nanny.

In order to keep things running smoothly between you and your nanny, implementing a few expectations at the beginning of your relationship will help you avoid problems in the future. We have touched on these topics earlier in this book, but we will review the most important tasks now:

- A Daily Check-In

- Scheduling a Monthly Meeting

- Scheduling Performance Evaluations – at 3 months, 6 months, and 1 year

## A Daily Check-In

Earlier we covered the baby journal and how important it is to your peace of mind. Knowing what happens in your child's life on a daily basis keeps you emotionally connected, even when you are out of the home. An excellent resource for jogging your memory on what is important to you is a comprehensive childcare organizer by Melissa Bishop & Karen Berg titled *The Caregiver Organizer For MY Child* [6].

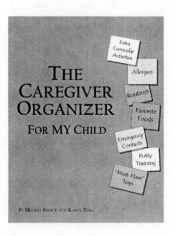

This is a wonderful guide that covers everything to empower your nanny to create a smooth running routine. Organized in sections, with reproducible guides, *The Caregiver Organizer* helps you:

- Share each child's daily routine, likes, and dislikes with your nanny
- Prepare your sitter and your family for any emergency situation
- Organize your child's medical information in one place
- Run your household when you are not there and locate items in your home
- Keep all important phone numbers in one place
- Keep track of medical issues and behavior patterns

---

6  *The Caregiver Organizer For MY Child (www.bythebookkids.com)*

This is a wonderful tool to keep yourself organized while you are away from your home. What is great about *The Caregiver Organizer* is that it reminds you of all the things you want to tell your nanny but have forgotten in your rush to get to work.

Whatever method you choose to keep track of what is going on in your child's life, set up the practice of daily written reports to keep yourself well informed of what is going on in your child's life.

## A Monthly Meeting

Much less formal than a performance evaluation, a monthly meeting gives you and your nanny the opportunity to review the good and challenging aspects of the childcare situation in a relaxed setting. It is your opportunity to correct any habits or behavior that you don't agree with and lets your nanny clear the air as well. This meeting should be between you and your nanny without your child present. Of course, if any issues come up in between meetings, it's always best to handle things when they occur.

## Performance Evaluations

Having regularly scheduled performance evaluations at one month, three months, six months, and one year is a way to keep unsatisfactory behaviors from getting out of control. In even the most ideal situations, it is not possible for you and your nanny to know everything about each other at the beginning of your relationship. It is much better to correct any behavior in the daily reports than to blow up in anger on some subsequent evaluation date over a mistake that occurred months prior.

If you haven't provided your nanny with a written job description and a list of the essential tasks for which she is responsible, now is the time. You will be referring to this document in the future to evaluate her performance. It is unfair to hold someone accountable for tasks that are unexplained, so make this a working document. For example, if ironing a child's party dress is important to you, ironing should be included under the task, "being responsible for the child's laundry."

An evaluation should break down assignments by category. Your nanny may be responsible for many tasks, but three categories usually cover most circumstances: childcare, housekeeping and work habits. Since a performance evaluation is designed to praise your nanny for excellent work and improve any areas that you are not happy with, create a five point scale that goes from poor (1), satisfactory (3) to excellent (5). With this system you can provide positive feedback and improve results. Design an evaluation that you will use for each step during the first year and then move to an annual evaluation.

Your daily log book will be a great help to both of you in preparing for an evaluation. Be sure you give your nanny notice that the evaluations are going to be held at a scheduled day and time. It is important that both parents be there if at all possible, and you will need to make arrangements for the care of the child, who should not be in attendance. A sample evaluation is included in the Appendix.

Depending on how you have scheduled your pay, it is appropriate to give small incentive raises, 2 to 4% at the evaluation times and a merit raise of 5 to 10% on the one year anniversary. Keep this in mind as you create your work agreement with your nanny.

A performance evaluation is not the time to bring up new issues. It is a time to review performance on issues that you have discussed on an ongoing basis with your nanny. No one likes to be surprised, and you will get your best performance from your nanny if you point out areas of correction when the problem occurs, not three months later.

At the evaluation, your nanny should be able to make a statement about how she sees her performance as well. Try to regard her feedback as just that: issues that make it more difficult for her to do her job. Each of you should sign the evaluation, and the nanny should receive a copy for her records.

*Section Five*

# Tips on Co-Existing with Your Nanny

# Top 10 Common Complaints of Nannies

The nanny-parent relationship is a unique one. A person comes into your life to provide care and nurturing for your child and is also present when you are at your best and worst. Nannies4hire. com surveyed nannies and babysitters about their working conditions. In response to the question, "What would you change about the parents?", 2,096 respondents raised the following issues:

| | |
|---|---|
| Not enough discipline with children | 24% |
| Not involved with the children | 20% |
| Inconsistent discipline with children | 19% |
| Showing anger to the children | 9% |
| Not following the rules | 4% |
| Trying to buy love from the children | 4% |
| Abusive to children | 4% |
| Poor communication | 2% |
| Neglecting children | 2% |
| Overprotective | 2% |

We also wanted to know what the challenges were today with caring for children. The issues most important to the nannies were the children's manners and respect for adults and a desire for them to read more and use technology less. Most nannies feel that the children in their care are a reflection of their parents' beliefs and attitudes.

One consistent problem that nannies mentioned is when parents do not agree on a subject, whether it is discipline, eating habits or bed times. For your nanny to do her best job, it is important for you and your partner to present a united front when it comes to issues relating to the children.

The following chart shows how much time children are spending in front of the television or computer screens, and listening to music and playing video games on a daily basis. A recent study by the Kaiser Family Foundation (2010) revealed that most children ages 8 to 18 are plugged into media on average 7.5 hours a day. Our survey shows that children supervised by a nanny only spend 1.6 hours a day engaging with media and on average 3 hours a day playing outside.

## DAILY MEDIA USE BY CHILDREN AGES 8–18 WITH NANNY VS. NATIONAL AVERAGE

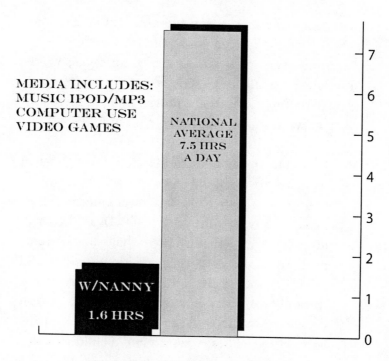

MEDIA INCLUDES:
MUSIC IPOD/MP3
COMPUTER USE
VIDEO GAMES

NATIONAL
AVERAGE
7.5 HRS
A DAY

W/NANNY

1.6 HRS

7
6
5
4
3
2
1
0

2010 Survey NANNIES4HIRE.COM
NATIONAL AVERAGE KAISER FAMILY FOUNDATION

## *Candi's Take on Parenting Mistakes*

Parenting requires a considerable amount of on-the-job training, and most of us feel like we're learning every day. We all make mistakes; we're human, after all, but when we strive to improve our parenting skills, our children benefit. Here are just a few mistakes that parents often make:

- **Giving In** - It can be *hard* to follow through when it comes to discipline, but it's so important. If you ground your child for a week because they broke a certain rule, stick to it. Don't let them go play with friends later that day. Parents need to make sure their children understand rules, expectations, and consequences. Sure, it would be easier *not* to deal with the crayon drawings on the wall or other infraction of the rules; no one likes to reprimand a child for poor behavior!  But if you're clear about the rules and consequences, your child will quickly learn the difference between right and wrong...and they will ultimately respect you for teaching important life lessons.

- **Giving Too Much** - These days, we give our children a lot of stuff, which leads to wanting more. When they're already overloaded with toys, a new one won't seem special. Try giving experiences as treats, rewards, or to celebrate special occasions. If your daughter comes home with a stellar report card, take her for a special bike ride or a walk in the park. Experiences with you are *far* more valuable than the latest toy.

- **Over-Scheduling Your Child** - Extracurricular activities are wonderful and teach your child important skills, but over-scheduling can backfire. If you're constantly shuffling your child from Girl Scouts to dance recitals to piano practice, your child won't have enough downtime to just...play. Give your child time to use their imagination. They don't have to be scheduled every moment of every day.

- **Not Asking Questions** - Learn more about your children and constantly improve your relationship with them by asking questions about their day, their friends, and what happened at school. Make sure they know they can tell you or ask you anything.

- **Disrespecting Your Child** - Model all the behaviors that you expect of your child. Be nice, watch your words when you're upset, don't yell or call your child names, and use good manners.

sixteen

# A Look at Some Nanny Situations

**Temporary Nannies**

Some families may find that they need a nanny only for temporary situations, such as an illness or recovering from surgery, on summer vacation, or on winter vacation. If you are in need of temporary services, you may find that our sister company, Care-4hire.com is a better fit. Caregivers indicate if they are available for part-time or temporary work, night care, or emergency care. As with most things, it is better to be prepared before an event occurs. Take the time to create a list of local caregivers to be used in the event of an emergency. Do not take shortcuts in checking the references and backgrounds of even temporary workers as they will be in your life when you are the most vulnerable.

**Vacation Nannies**

Parents can save money and travel expenses by hiring a nanny at their vacation site. The nannies are usually local, which can add great value to your vacation: they go home at night so you have your privacy in the evenings. You can look for a local agency which has already checked references and completed a background check, or you can use an online service like Care-4hire.com which has a comprehensive database for the United States and Canada which is much more cost effective.

## Needing Your Nanny: Candi's Take on Mommy Guilt

No parent wants to stick their child in front of a computer or video game when they have been with a nanny all day. What's a mom to do when she also faces a deadline at work? It's a struggle that many of us face: running a household while running off to work. Sometimes the sheer volume of tasks that we have to accomplish, from leading a staff meeting to leading the Cub Scout troop, is just staggering.

Here are some tips to help you feel more in control:

- Empower your children to be independent. Let them choose their own healthy snacks, outfits, and so forth. You won't be sweating the small stuff, and your children will be delighted with the responsibility that you've given them.

- Embrace your imperfections. So you didn't serve a home-cooked meal tonight. Who cares? Serve your frozen lasagna with a smile.

- Focus on work while you're at work and on home when you're at home. Don't worry about your emails, to-do lists, and pending meetings while you're spending time with your children. Likewise, don't worry about your children while you're at work. You've left them in capable, loving care, so focus on your work and get it done so you can get home to them.

- Force yourself to disconnect. In today's age of laptops, iPhones®, and Blackberries®, you're always accessible and "on the clock." Learn that it's OK to shut down all of your electronics to play board games, help with homework, or go for a walk with your child.

- Hire your child as your assistant. Occasionally I need to work while I'm home with my children. They used to pout about it until I hired them to help me. I give them special projects, like filling the paper tray on my printer, sharpening my pencils and even supervised paper shredding. They also enjoy doing paperwork (coloring or workbooks) at their desks, while I work at mine.

## A Day In The Life Of A Live-In Nanny

*In Candi's Own Words: A Typical Day for a Live-in Nanny Caring for a Family with Five Children (Candi's first job was as a nanny for five children, including twins. This is her recollection of that time.)*

**Interviewer: *Candi, can you tell us about a normal day for you with the children?***

In my nanny position, there were five children. Two of the children, ages five and seven, were in school, and the three-year-old and newborn twins stayed at home. On a normal day, I would wake up before the older kids, make them breakfast, and then help them get dressed and off to school. Depending on the day, we would either walk to school, which was close by, or their mom would drive them, and then I would usually stay home with the younger kids. In this family, the mom was very active, and she would be involved in volunteer work, or she'd go to the gym and work out every day. On most days, I was home with the kids all day.

They were a very busy family, and I filled in wherever I was needed. The mom and I worked as a team. There would be times that I'd run to the grocery store for her or we'd run out to the mall together if we needed something for the kids. The family and kids were very social, so one of my responsibilities was to manage the events like birthday parties for the kids. I would do the birthday gift shopping on my own or with the older children. It was my responsibility to get the gifts wrapped and have the children ready to go to the party.

Much of my experience was staying home with the twins as well. Because they were so little, the parents didn't want them to be out in public. I helped them with everything they needed. With five children, someone always needed something, and I was there to fill that need. I know many nannies help with the heavy housekeeping, but they had a cleaning lady that came in two times a week as well.

Interviewer: *Did you prepare any meals?*
I did all the meal preparation for the kids and then, on top of that, I would help start the family meals as well, or I would help make a salad or whatever they needed that night. When I first got there, the mom was still pregnant and was on bed rest with the twins. She wasn't able to do a lot, so very quickly I took on many household jobs, like cooking, picking up after the kids and taking them out for their activities.

Interviewer: *And with the kids—how did they accept the new twins' arrival?*
The youngest one, the three-year-old, was a rambunctious little boy; the other two were girls, the five- and seven-year-olds. Of the twins, there was one boy and one girl. The three older kids did

very well accepting the twins. The three-year-old went through his times where he was testy, but overall, I think the kids were accepting of the twins. I think it also helped that the mom was a stay-at-home mom. I was an extra pair of hands helping out.

Interviewer: *Is that the norm: for mom to be at home?*
No, for the majority of nanny jobs, moms are not at home.

Interviewer: *Is there a difference between the two situations; Moms at Home VS Working Moms?*
There's a huge difference, because when you are a nanny and the mom is at home, you're an extension of the mom. She is usually the one who makes the moment-to-moment decisions. She is still the decision-maker. When you are a nanny and the mom is at work, you're the decision-maker.

Interviewer: *When you're the extra pair of hands, are you waiting to be told what to do?*
At first, you are looking for more direction, but as time passes, you know the role and what needs to be done. For my situation, at first she gave me more direction, but as time went on, I just knew what to do with the kids and what else needed to be done.

Interviewer: *Were there any areas that the mom was really focused on, where things had to be done a particular way?*
You know, not that I really recall. I always had a routine with the kids. I worked Monday through Friday and had the weekends off. The family trusted my judgment, and I knew how the mom liked things done. I never felt restricted or controlled in any way.

**Interviewer:** *Did anything unusual happen while you were caring for the children?*
There was one time when the parents were away; it was kind of a funny story. My mom came out and helped me with the twins because the family was going out of town skiing. My mom and I were out shopping at the mall. I was young; maybe 19 years old. This lady came up to me and said, "Oh, my goodness, you did this?" She pointed to the twins like I had these twins! At 19! Wow! She knew the babies couldn't be my mom's but they could be mine. I guess when you're strolling around with twins; people usually think you're the mom. I was with the twins almost 20 years ago, and multiples were always a big deal then. Today, multiples are more frequent because of all the infertility treatments that result in multiple births.

**Interviewer:** *As a live-in nanny, did you have your privacy?*
I had my own room with a private bath attached to it. That is common for a live-in nanny. There are occasions that nannies will just have their own room, and they will have a shared bathroom. Often, when you are a live-in nanny, you never get time away because, on your days off, you're still there. Even though you are "not on working hours," it's, like, how do you get that time away? And I know, overall, you hear a lot of nannies that say, "Gosh, sometimes on my days off I just go hang out at the mall. I just go do something just to get out of the house." If not, you're in the house so much of the day.

**Interviewer:** *Were you called to work on the weekends?*

Usually, you don't have to get up and do your job, but what stops the kids from coming up and saying, "Would you help me with this?" or "What's this?" When I was younger, the kids would definitely come up and see what I was doing or come and see if I would help them with something. I didn't mind. They definitely treated me like I was a part of their family.

**Interviewer:** *And did you eat your meals with them?*
I did. I ate my meals with them. They really treated me like I was a part of the family.

**Interviewer:** *Did you have a separate car?*
I took my own car out there. I had my own car so that I could go as I pleased on my days off.

**Interviewer:** *And what about when you were driving their kids?*
When I drove their kids, I used their car. Often, that's how it works. If a nanny is transporting the children in her car, the family would be responsible for paying mileage.

**Interviewer:** *How long did you stay on the job?*
I stayed one year, and then I was ready to get back home.

seventeen

# Sticky Business

### Accidents Happen: When Is "I'm Sorry" Enough?

Your nanny accidentally spilled something on your new sofa. Or she broke a valuable vase. She apologized and was sincerely sorry.

But what if she was involved in a more upsetting indiscretion? She invited her boyfriend over while she was watching your child, when your policy clearly prohibits this. Or she smoked in front of your child, which violates your healthy living values. Or she let your young child bike unsupervised in the road, while she was inside chatting on the phone. When you caught her, she said she was sorry, but, in these situations, is an apology enough?

Hiring a nanny involves a lot of trust. As the parent, you need to feel comfortable that she's following your rules, instilling your values, and focusing all of her energy on caring for your child. And when she violates this trust, is an apology good enough? Or do you need to find a more responsible nanny?

## Candi's Take on Apologies

I'm a big fan of open communication between parents and caregivers, and I believe it's important to be clear from the beginning about your rules. It's totally valid to prohibit your nanny from having guests over, smoking, or talking on the phone for hours unless your child is sleeping. Her job is to watch your children and keep them safe, so if you find out that your four-year-old was out biking in the road while the nanny was inside for an hour, it's time to find a new caregiver. It's up to you, as the parents, to decide which behaviors are forgivable. If she broke your vase, it was clearly an accident. But if she broke your trust, an apology probably won't be enough.

### Crossing Boundaries - Nanny Cam

A nanny cam is a hidden video camera designed to record the behavior of your nanny while you are away from home. The use of a nanny cam is legal in all 50 states, if you tell your nanny that she has no right to expect privacy in your home. If you choose to use a video cam, it is best to have your nanny sign a statement that she knows she will be videotaped in your home. Check with your attorney if you decide to use a nanny cam or audio recording, the latter being illegal in 15 states.

## *Candi's Take on Nanny Cams*

The idea of having a "nanny cam", a hidden camera, has become quite controversial in recent years. Some parents think it's a great way to keep track of their children and their nannies, while others think it's a blatant invasion of privacy. Further, some parents are up front about the device, telling their caretaker that they will be using the camera to check in periodically. Others risk legal challenges and use it secretly to ensure that their nanny is taking proper care of their children.

As long as parents aren't taping footage of nannies without their consent, nanny cams are legal in all 50 states. But here's the moral dilemma: Should parents tell nannies where they have nanny cams hidden? Many parents are using cameras hidden in teddy bears, houseplants, clocks, etc. to keep tabs on their children... as well as their nannies. Is this smart parenting or an invasion of privacy?

## Consider the following:

- Have you told your nanny about the camera and use it in a positive way - to see what your child is doing rather than keeping tabs on what your *nanny* is doing? Do you check in throughout the day to see your cute child playing? Or...

- Are you keeping your "nanny cam" a secret because you don't trust your childcare provider? Has she given you any reason to question her capabilities? Are you worried over news reports about nannies harming babies and want to covertly watch her behavior?

In my line of work, I hear arguments on both sides of the debate. I always encourage honesty between parents and their nannies, and urge parents to hire nannies that they trust to take great care of their children. If parents have any reason to doubt their nannies, I recommend that they sit down and have a discussion about these concerns. I counsel them to trust their instincts: if they're still uncomfortable about something even after talking to their nanny about it, then it's time to consider other childcare options.

## Confidentiality Agreements

You don't have to be famous to need an agreement to protect your family and work conversations from being repeated by your nanny. In general, a confidentiality agreement will prevent your nanny from repeating conversations overheard about or between your family members and the people that may visit your home casually or at a party. The agreement puts your nanny on notice that you own all information concerning your family and prohibits the nanny from sharing your private information with anyone. A well crafted document establishes your nanny's loyalty to the family and lays out the actions that can be taken if the trust is broken.

In today's media-mad society, a confidentiality agreement will explain how or if the nanny should interact with the media and press, as well as the consequences if the policy is violated. It will also lay out what happens in the event the employee is terminated down the road. It is best to check with an attorney on how to draft a confidentiality agreement.

## Your Nanny Is My Nanny: When Friends Take Advantage of Your Good Fortune

We all know that it takes a village to raise a child, and we're (mostly) happy to help out our fellow parents on occasion, with the understanding that they'll return the favor when we need help. But what happens when your friend, sister, neighbor, or fellow elementary school mom starts taking advantage of your good nature, dropping off her children at your house while she runs errands, goes to the gym, or gets a manicure? I know. It's *so infuriating!*

- Explain your feelings. Perhaps she doesn't realize that she's taking advantage of you. She may think that, as a stay-at-home mom, you're "home anyway," without realizing that you have things to do - and watching her adorable little munchkins distracts you from your busy agenda. Or she may think that since "you have a nanny anyway," she can drop off *her* children and your sitter will watch them for free.

- Offer a "kid swap" - You scratch her back, and she should scratch yours. Propose a kid swap where, say, you take turns watching each others' kids every Wednesday afternoon.

- Offer a solution. Give her the name of a reliable babysitting or nanny service, like Care4hire.com or Nannies4hire.com and suggest she hire someone to watch her children, as your schedule won't permit you to continue to do so.

- Have an excuse ready. If she still doesn't get the hint, have an excuse ready when her children show up at your doorstep. "Gee, I'd love to have you stay here today, but I have to run errands/paint my attic/ reorganize my closet and I just won't be able to do it today. Sorry." And shut the door!

# eighteen

# Nannies and Social Networking Websites

### Should I Be My Nanny's Friend?

The old adage says you shouldn't judge a book by its cover, but many of us still do so, at least on occasion. We all have an image in our minds of what the "ideal" nanny should look like, and that image is probably more Mary Poppins than Marilyn Manson. You're probably envisioning pink sweaters, not Pink the rock star.

When it comes to nannies, would you hire someone with visible body piercings, tattoos, a mohawk hairstyle, a punk-rock style, etc.? Tattoos and body piercings have become increasingly popular in recent years. Some of this body art is, of course, hidden from view, but others are in plain sight. Many people are completely in favor of these forms of self-expression. Further, they believe that nannies, like all of us, are entitled to live their own lives: and as long as they're great with children, who cares about the artwork on their bodies?

These folks base their decision about hiring a caregiver on other criteria that they deem more important, such as the potential nanny's experience, references, personality, interests, availability, and salary requirements. They may also view this as an opportunity to teach their children valuable lessons about diversity and how it's OK to look *different*. Others view tattoos and piercings with disdain, thinking that it's inappropriate and unprofessional, especially for those in the childcare industry. They believe that nannies should look and act appropriately and they have a definite point of view about what is and isn't appropriate. Also, they may view their nanny as an extension of their family and prefer this family representative to have a more professional appearance.

Are you comfortable hiring a sitter with body piercings or tattoos? Does image matter to you? Do you or your partner have tattoos and body piercings? And, perhaps most importantly, do you think that your opinion on this subject will influence how your child views and judge people?

These questions become more and more important as you delve into the private world of social media, a major communication vehicle for the 20-something generation. Social media websites like Twitter, Facebook and MySpace have sunk their fair share of careers in the corporate world. Do they play a role in your world? The answer to that question is yes and no. When checking out your nanny, there are two elements to consider: their public persona and their private world. Inappropriate pictures, names, and comments on the public listing may indicate a level of immaturity and poor judgment. Asking to become a social network friend is more like reading your nanny's personal diary. When communicating with their real friends, the conversations are more likely to be casual and unguarded. Think back on the things you did and said in your twenties. Would you have passed your parents' test if they had known your most intimate thoughts? Probably not. The details on your nanny's social networking most likely fall into the category of 'over share'. It's fine to talk to your nanny about their online presence, but unless they are constantly online or texting their friends while on duty, it really is their business.

# conclusion

In today's society, finding quality childcare is important to so many families, no matter where you live. Here are some of the most important things for you to consider when selecting a new nanny for your child.

1. The nanny should be able to relate easily and bond well with your child while also maintaining a clear distinction from them. A nanny must be able to play with and enjoy your child, which can often be construed by the child as peer-level interaction, while also maintaining discipline. It is easy for a nanny and a parent to feel more comfortable in one role or the other: to be most comfortable being friends with the child, or to be most comfortable supervising the child and redirecting their errant behaviors. Parents and nannies must have a shared understanding of how to navigate both roles successfully and strike a balance between peer-level interaction and parent-level interaction with the child.

2. The nanny must be able to relate with your family and administer discipline to your child in a manner that is appropriate and consistent with your family's boundaries. You and your nanny should discuss, prior to hiring, the discipline style that your family would like the nanny to use.

3.  The nanny should have years of experience, solid references from prior employer-families, a clean background (pursuant to background checks), and completed training on nanny basics: CPR, first aid, the Heimlich maneuver, basic nutrition and food preparation, and general personal and home hygiene. Background checks may be obtained through Nannies4hire.com. If you need your nanny to drive, then your nanny should have a valid driver's license and a clean or as close to clean as possible driving record.

4.  The nanny should be able to develop and carry out fun, creative, and educational experiences for your child.

5.  The nanny should be capable of handling small crises on her own. You and your nanny should come to an agreement about what issues may warrant a call to you and what issues the nanny is authorized to handle on her own. Your nanny should be able to act comfortably within the boundaries you have provided.

6.  The nanny should be able to commit to your family for an extended period of time, unless your circumstances require less. Children often become attached to their nannies. When nannies leave, children often experience grief associated with that separation. Therefore, it is advantageous to hire a nanny who will be able to stay with your child for an extended amount of time.

7.  The nanny's expectations regarding terms and conditions of employment should be close to the terms and conditions of employment that you

are offering. If you are seeking a live-in nanny, a prospective nanny that seeks a live-out arrangement may not be a good fit for your family. If you wish to hire a nanny in a smoking home, a non-smoking prospective nanny may not be a good fit for your family. Pay rates for nannies should be discussed up front to ensure that the prospective nannies are willing to work for the income you offer.

8. The nanny should not have fears or concerns about the non-negotiable aspects of the job with your family. If you have a cat, and your prospective nanny is severely allergic to cats, the prospective nanny may not be a good fit for your family. (Side note: some allergic reactions can be treated with over-the-counter or prescription medications or other accommodations that may be used by the allergic nanny.)

9. The nanny should be a positive, loving influence in your household.

Childhood is a time of growth, unconditional love and wonder. It will be over sooner than you can ever imagine. By creating a safe and happy world with the help of a nanny, your child will have the best of both worlds: a stress-free time of growing up with happy parents. Remember, your nanny is your best defense in keeping your child happy, healthy and excited about life while you take care of the business of earning a living.

# Selected Bibliography

Ahlers, Joan and Cheryl Tallman, *All About Me Diary, The Ultimate Record of Your Child's Day,* National Book Network, Lanham, MD, 2004, www.Freshbaby.com

Ban Breathnach, Sarah, *The Victorian Nursery Companion,* Simon & Schuster, New York, NY 1992, www.simpleabundance.com

Berg, Karen & Bishop, Melissa, *The Caregiver Organizer For MY Child*, Karmel Publishing, St. Louis, MO 2007, www.bythebookkids.com

Budd, Linda S., *Living with the Alert Active Child*, Prentice Publishing, New York, NY 1990

Chess, M.D., Stella and Mahin Hassibi, M.D., *Principles and Practices of Child Psychiatry,* Springer Publishing, New York, NY, 1978

Healthy Steps for Young Children, National Initiative, The Commonwealth Fund; Boston University School of Medicine; American Academy of Pediatrics; Healthy Steps National Advisory Committee, April, 2006, http://www.commonwealthfund.org/Content/Innovations/Tools/2006/Apr/Healthy-Steps-Preventive-Care-for-Young-Children.aspx

Kurcinka, Mary Sheedy. *Raising Your Spirited Child*, Harper Paperbacks, New York, NY 1998

Maddalone,Guy. *How To Hire A Nanny: A Household HR™ Handbook* http://www.gtm.com Illinois: Sphinx® Publishing, 2007

Mayo Clinc – © 1998-2009 Mayo Foundation for Medical Education and Research (MFMER), Infant Development, Birth to Three Months

PEDIATRICS, Vol. 122, No. 5 November 2008, pp. e980-987

Sears, Martha and Dr. William, *Parenting the Fussy Baby and the High Needs Child*, Little Brown & Co, Boston, MA 1996

Thomas, Alexander, Stella Chess and Herbert Birth, *New York Longitudinal Study on Personality traits and Temperament*, 1956

Turecki M.D.,Stanley with Leslie Tonner, *The Difficult Child*, Expanded and Revised Edition, Bantam, New York, NY, 2000

United States: Federal Equal Employment Opportunity (EEO) Laws, November, 2009 http://www.eeoc.gov/facts/qanda.html

# Additional References

The Henry J. Kaiser Family Foundation, *Generation M2: Media in the Lives of 8- to 18-Year-Olds*, 2010

GTM Payroll Services, www.gtm.com

International Nanny Association website, www.nanny.org

Neuro-Linguistic Programming developed by Dr. Richard Bandler and John Grinder

# Appendix

# Nannies4hire.com Sample Contract

Agreement between _____(employer) and _____ (employee)

01. Date of hire: _____to_____

02. Full-time childcare positions require the following responsibilities:
    a. To provide childcare ____ hours per day ____ days per week
    b. Please circle work days: Mon Tues Wed Thurs Fri Sat Sun
    c. Please circle days off each week:
       Mon Tues Wed Thurs Fri Sat Sun

03. To plan and prepare nutritious meals and snacks for the children.

04. To plan and carry out activities to encourage social, physical, emotional and intellectual development of the child(ren).

05. Additional responsibilities (Please check the duties for which your nanny will be responsible on a regular or daily basis):

| Duties | Daily | Every Other Day | Weekly |
|---|---|---|---|
| a. Children's meal preparation | ____ | ____ | ____ |
| Breakfast | ____ | ____ | ____ |
| Morning snack | ____ | ____ | ____ |
| Lunch | ____ | ____ | ____ |
| Afternoon snack | ____ | ____ | ____ |
| Dinner | ____ | ____ | ____ |
| Bedtime snack | ____ | ____ | ____ |
| b. Cleaning children's dishes | | | |
| Breakfast | ____ | ____ | ____ |
| Morning snack | ____ | ____ | ____ |
| Lunch | ____ | ____ | ____ |
| Afternoon snack | ____ | ____ | ____ |
| Dinner | ____ | ____ | ____ |
| Bedtime snack | ____ | ____ | ____ |

c. Employer's bedroom &
   private sitting room
   Picked up                    ____      ____      ____
   Bed made                     ____      ____      ____

d. Employer's meal preparation  ____      ____      ____

e. Employer's dishes            ____      ____      ____

f. Meal planning &
   grocery shopping
   Children only                ____      ____      ____
   Family                       ____      ____      ____
   Employee's                   ____      ____      ____

g. Vacuuming
   Children's bedrooms          ____      ____      ____
   Children's playrooms         ____      ____      ____
   Employee's private rooms     ____      ____      ____
   Entire home                  ____      ____      ____

h. Dusting
   Children's bedrooms          ____      ____      ____
   Children's playrooms         ____      ____      ____
   Employee's private rooms     ____      ____      ____
   Entire home                  ____      ____      ____

i. Cleaning Bathrooms           ____      ____      ____
   Children's bedrooms          ____      ____      ____
   Children's playrooms         ____      ____      ____
   Employee's private rooms     ____      ____      ____
   Entire home                  ____      ____      ____

j. General Picking up home
   Children's bedrooms          ____      ____      ____
   Children's playrooms         ____      ____      ____
   Employee's private rooms     ____      ____      ____
   Entire home                  ____      ____      ____

k. Laundry
   Children's                   ____      ____      ____

Employee's ___   ___   ___
Family's ___   ___   ___

l.  Miscellaneous tasks
    Packing lunch – children
    Packing lunch – family         ___   ___   ___

    Ironing – children
    Ironing – family               ___   ___   ___

    Taking out trash – children
    Taking out trash – family       ___   ___   ___

    Making dental/drs appts
    Children only
    Family                          ___   ___   ___
    Taking care of
    sick children                   ___   ___   ___

m.  Driving
    Children activities
    Family errands                  ___   ___   ___

n.  Periodic heavy cleaning
    In house as listed _____

o.  Tutoring_____

06.  Work schedule
    Monday      ___to ___      Thursday    ___to___
    Tuesday     ___to ___      Friday      ___to___
    Wednesday   ___to ___      Saturday    ___to ___
                               Sunday      ___to ___

    Up to ____ average hours per day, with the total not to exceed 50
    hours per week

    Over ____ hours a week will be paid $ ____ per hour

07.  Compensation
    a.  Employer agrees to pay the employee  $ ____ gross a week,
        $ ____net per week

    b. Salary is to be paid on _____(day) covering the time
       period of _____ weeks

08.  Twenty-four hour duty defined as:
    a. Twenty-four hour duty occurring during two normal workdays
       will be compensated as follows:_____

    b. Twenty-four hour duty occurring during one or more scheduled
       days off will be compensated as follows: _____

09.  Out-of-town duty, described as non-optional, regular working
    responsibilities while traveling with the family.

    a. While specific hours may vary, the number of working hours is
       per day, not to exceed _____.

    b. All travel expenses are to be paid by the employer, except those
       the employee elects to incur.

    c. Private accommodations ____will ____ will not be provided by
       the employer.

    d. Normal compensation ____will ____will not be provided by the
       employer.

    e. Hours worked, days off and compensation levels will be in
       accordance with the at-home policies (listed in this agreement),
       unless changes are listed below:_____

10.  Payroll taxes and any other taxes required by local, state or federal
    laws are to be agreed upon between the family and nanny and are
    the responsibility of the family and/or nanny and in no way will be
    the responsibility of Nannies4hire.com.

11.  Vacation
    a. Employer agrees to allow the employee ____ week(s) paid
       vacation to be taken as follows: ____as employer desires; or after
       ____ months of employment.
    b. Employee ____will ____will not be paid full salary if family
       travels without employee.

    c. Employer agrees to allow the employee _____ days/weeks paid sick leave.

12. Holiday
    a. Employer agrees to allow the employee the following paid holidays:_____

13. Health Insurance
    a. _____ paid by employer

    b. _____ percent of policy up to $_____/year paid by employer

    c. _____ no health insurance provided

14. Automobile provided
    a. _____for occasional personal use. Limited to _____ days/week

    b. _____for regular use with permission of employer

    c. _____for regular use without need for employer's permission

    d. _____work-related use only

    e. _____not offered, but use of employee's car for work-related errands will be compensated at _____/mile.

    f. Public Transportation Description:
    _____

    g. Auto insurance will be paid by the employer with _____ deductible

    h. _____ no automobile provided

15. Room and Board
    a. Shall be provided for the nanny (including all meals, snacks and other foods consumed by the nanny. Food shall be compatible to nanny's eating habits).
    b. _____no room and board provided

16. Accommodations and use of property
   a. Areas considered the employee's private accommodations are as follows _____

   b. ____ no accommodations for the employee

   c. Such designated areas ____ are ____are not open to any of the employee's guests without employer permission.
   _____

   d. Such designated areas ____will ____will not be cleaned by household staff.
   _____

   e. Common areas are areas open to all and are as follows:
   _____

   f. Common areas are to be used by employee as follows:
   ____ at any time
   ____ whenever not previously occupied by employer or employers guests
   ____ whenever employer is not at home

   g. Common areas may be used to entertain employee's guests as follows:
   ____ at any time
   ____ when not previously occupied by employer (without permission)
   ____ when employer is not at home (without permission)
   ____ with employer's permission only
   ____ not to be used by employee to entertain guests

   h. Telephone: Nanny will have use of:
   ____ shared line
   ____ private line paid by employer
   ____ private line paid by employee

   i. Curfew and other restrictions: _____

17. Respect of private areas and private property:
    a. Both employer and employee will respect the privacy of the other by knocking and awaiting invitation before entering any private areas.

    b. Employer has the right to enter employee's private areas; however, advance notice will be given whenever possible.

    c. All private property requiring special operating instructions will be available for use only after permission and instructions given.

    d. Private property not to be operated by employer or employee is as follows:

    _____

18. Other benefits offered:_____

19. The ____ family ____ nanny is responsible for transportation costs to the job. The ____ family ____ nanny is responsible for return transportation costs at the end of the commitment period.

20. Termination of Contract: This contract is an employment-at-will agreement. Employer and Employee may terminated the contract at any time, with or without cause, however:

    a. If the employee is terminated without cause, the employer is obligated to pay ____ weeks' severance pay.

    b. If the employee decides to leave the position with cause, the employee will provide ____ weeks notice, or if requested remain until a replacement nanny is found. No severance pay is required if employer wishes to terminate before the ____ week notice period.

Employee and Employer hereby acknowledge and warrant that Employer and Employee have given or provided full, complete and truthful information.

_____     _____
Employer's Signature/Date                         Employee Signature/Date

# Nannies4hire.com Nanny Evaluation

| Qualities | Very Satisfied | Satisfied | Less Than Satisfied | Required Improvement |
|---|---|---|---|---|
| Time Management | | | | |
| Initiative: | | | | |
|   Household Chores | | | | |
|   Children's Activities | | | | |
|   Personal Growth | | | | |
| Use Of Creativity | | | | |
| Respect For Employers' Privacy | | | | |
| Self-Motivation (ability to set goals, objectives, & plans) | | | | |
| Independence (ability to work & plan independently) | | | | |
| Nanny's Use Of Personal Time | | | | |
| Nanny's Relationship With:   Children   Parents   Peers | | | | |
| Ability To Accept Criticism & Make Changes | | | | |

# Nannies4hire.com Nanny Evaluation (cont'd)

| Qualities | Very Satisfied | Satisfied | Less Than Satisfied | Required Improvement |
|---|---|---|---|---|
| Ability To Communicate With Employer | | | | |
| Displays Positive Attitude | | | | |
| Awareness Of Children's Needs | | | | |
| Follows Family's Discipline Style | | | | |
| Effectiveness Of Nanny's Discipline | | | | |
| Provide Reasonable Flexibility In Emergency & Unexpected Schedule Changes | | | | |
| Matching Family's Housekeeping Standards | | | | |
| Meal Planning & Preparation | | | | |
| Nanny's Appearance: | | | | |
| Task Appropriate Attire | | | | |
| Cleanliness | | | | |
| Neatness | | | | |

# nannies4hire.com™

## For Further Information

Candi Wingate would like to hear from you about your experience with hiring your nanny. Candi can be reached at:

> Nannies4hire.com
> P.O. Box 2202
> Norfolk, NE 68702
> (402) 379-4121

We invite you to try a free nanny or caregiver search at:

> www.nannies4hire.com
> www.care4hire.com
> www.babysitters4hire.com

Good luck with your search and we hope you find the right nanny for your family.

LaVergne, TN USA
19 December 2010
209377LV00004B/98/P

9 780982 698907